# Canvas of the Mind

Rajesh Dangi, 2024

*"In the vast gallery of the mind, emotions are the vibrant pigments, thoughts are the intricate brushstrokes, and the canvas, ever evolving, bears the masterpiece of our inner world."*

Table of contents

# Preface

Beneath the facade of our everyday existence lies a dynamic and pulsating tapestry of human experience, teeming with life's profound intricacies. This unseen canvas resonates with the vibrant energy of emotions, the spontaneous eruptions that add hues of joy, sorrow, or rage to the fabric of our every interaction. It is a living, breathing mural that captures the essence of what it means to be alive.

Within this context, delicate threads of feelings weave an intricate pattern, leaving lingering impressions on the canvas of our souls. These impressions are the subtle, subjective notes that echo in the corridors of our inner selves, shaping the unique melody of our personal narratives. They are the whispers that, though soft, wield profound influence over the harmony of our being.

Moods, akin to masterful strokes, paint broad canvases on this living artwork. They cast the world in warm, sunny hues of contentment, where every interaction feels like a sunlit embrace. Simultaneously, they can splash stormy greys of melancholy, transforming the very atmosphere around us into a tempest of introspection.

Woven seamlessly into this tapestry are the threads of sentiments—subtle inclinations and biases that subtly guide our judgments and tinge our interpretations of the world. They are the invisible ink that imprints our worldview, shaping the lens through which we perceive reality.

Our emotions and feelings, although intangible, find a tangible voice through expressions, the outward manifestations that become the brushstrokes of our shared language. Faces become canvases where joy, sorrow, love, and countless other emotions are painted. Eyes flicker like candle flames, revealing the depth of our innermost thoughts, and voices tremble, carrying the echoes of our emotional landscapes.

Yet, within this intricate tapestry, deeper strands bind us together. Passions, akin to fierce flames, propel us forward with an unyielding force, giving meaning and direction to our lives. These flames illuminate the path of desire and purpose, forging our unique journeys in the grand tapestry of existence.

Woven alongside passions are the gentle threads of affections and the bonds of love, empathy, and connection that form the very fabric of human society. They are the stitches that create a resilient tapestry, connecting us to one another in a symphony of shared experiences.

This is not just a collection of poetic thoughts or an invitation; it is a beckoning to help us explore the spectrum of our emotions, to unravel the knots of our feelings, to bask in the warm glow of our moods, and to decipher the whispers of our sentiments.

It's a celebration of the power of expressions and an ignition of the passionate embers within each of us. So, let us embark on this poetic journey together, peeling back the layers of our inner lives—one vibrant strand at a time so that we may authentically understand what it truly means to be human.

Rajesh Dangi

Bangalore India, Jan 2024

# Canvas of the Mind: Introduction

Close your eyes, not in sleep, but in a waking dream. Imagine a canvas, not spun from thread or carved from stone, but woven from moonlight and stardust, the whispers of windswept dreams where every heartbeat echoes like a brushstroke, every thought ripples like ink in a cosmic well. Here, in this realm where sunbeams dance with shadows and constellations of emotions shimmer, I invite you to wander with me..

## A Symphony of the Soul

A symphony of soul, Like a canvas vast,
Where hues of feeling bleed, honest and fast

Emotions rage, any storms that pass,
Sentiments like whispers, intertwine the mass...

Feeling's blush and metaphors haze,
While passions burn, in fervent gaze...

Ambition's fire, stories to be told.
Expressions dance, those akin and bold...

A fleeting smile, a tear unseen,
A laugh etched, wept Inside as keen...

Affections bloom, in gentle touch,
Bonds that hold, and means so much...

Anchoring moments within the mind,
joy, sigh, or ache, as the truth we find ...

Rhyme the heartbeat, to awaken the soul,
Embrace these moments and make it whole ...

## A Symphony of the Soul (Synopsys)

"A Symphony of the Soul" unfolds like a rich legacy, painting the intricate emotions and experiences that define the human journey. This poetic masterpiece captures the essence of the soul's symphony, where feelings burst forth in a kaleidoscope of hues.

The verses explore the raw authenticity of emotions, likening the soul to a vast canvas where feelings bleed forth with honesty and urgency. Storms of emotions pass through, leaving behind whispers that intricately intertwine, creating a mass of sentiments that echo like a symphony.

The poem delves into the nuanced shades of feelings, where blushes of emotion and metaphors blend seamlessly. Passion becomes a fervent gaze, while ambition ignites fires that fuel untold stories. Expressions dance boldly, crafting a narrative that is both familiar and daring.

Within the verses, fleeting smiles, unseen tears, and laughter etched with keenness illustrate the depth of human experience. Affections bloom in gentle touches, creating bonds that hold profound meaning. Moments, anchored within the mind, unravel in joy, sighs, or aches, revealing the truth of existence. The heartbeat becomes a rhyme, awakening the soul to embrace these moments and weave them into a harmonious whole. "A Symphony of the Soul" serves as a lyrical celebration of the multifaceted nature of human emotions, urging the reader to savour and embrace every note in the symphony of life.

# Beyond Labels: The Nuances of Inner Sensations

As you stand on the precipice of this metaphysical realm, let the enchanting imagery of the Canvas of the Mind give way to a contemplative lens. Imagine your consciousness as a canvas, a mental tableau upon which the brushstrokes of emotions, thoughts, and expressions coalesce to paint the intricate landscape of your inner world.

Within this context, the beat of your heart becomes the rhythmic cadence guiding the strokes of this internal masterpiece. Emotions, those vibrant hues, tango with the shadows of your thoughts, creating a nuanced chiaroscuro that shapes the contours of your being. It's a living canvas, ever-changing, ever-evolving, mirroring the ebb and flow of your experiences.

Consider, for a moment, the meticulous craft of this internal artist, i.e. the mind. Each sigh, a subtle brushstroke, etches a whisper of emotion onto the canvas. Doubt, a careful blending of charcoal tones against the luminescence of your dreams. Joy, a burst of golden light illuminating the recesses of your soul. In this analytical light, emotions take on the role of pigments, and the mind, the masterful hand that blends them into a coherent symphony of self-expression.

As you traverse this mental landscape, the wind of inspiration becomes the carrier of forgotten narratives, the seeds of untold stories waiting to germinate. Memory-laden meadows are the spaces where laughter blossoms like wildflowers, and the mountains of ambition are scaled, their peaks bathed in the fiery glow of passions.

Delve into the fathomless depths of introspection, where the coral reefs of your subconscious harbour secrets waiting to be unveiled. Analyze the tears that fall as cleansing rains, nurturing the soil of creativity. Here, every scar tells a story, a unique brushstroke adding depth and texture to the canvas. Mistakes are not flaws but intentional smudges that redefine the horizon, leading to uncharted territories of self-discovery.

## Beyond the Canvas, Within the Mind

Where brushstrokes dance and colors bind,
A canvas vast, the inner kind.
No earthly frame, no mortal hand,
This masterpiece on shifting sand.

Emotions swirl, a vibrant hue,
Joy's golden laugh, the morning dew.
Doubt's charcoal whispers, soft and grey,
Hope's sunrise paints the break of day.

Each sigh, a touch, a fleeting trace,
Etching stories on the mind's embrace.
Tears cleansed like rain, on fertile ground,
Where scars like brushstrokes, depth are found.

Memories bloom, wildflowers bright,
On hills of laughter, bathed in light.
Ambition climbs, a fiery quest,
On mountains forged within the breast.

The wind of whispers, secrets heard,
From stories whispered, never stirred.
Forgotten dreams, like seeds asleep,
In introspection's furrows deep.

No label binds, no line defines,
The boundless art the conscious mind designs.

A living landscape, ever free,
A symphony of you and me.

So let the colors bleed and blend,
In this masterpiece that has no end.
Embrace the light, the dark, the space,
The canvas yours, to paint with grace.

For in this realm, beyond the known,
The truest art is self-alone.

~

In this exploration, envision your mind as a dynamic canvas, responsive to the brushstrokes of your conscious and subconscious thoughts. As you navigate this mental landscape, you are not just an observer but an active participant, shaping the narrative of your inner world. The Canvas of the Mind, in this perspective, becomes a symbol of the ongoing interplay between emotions, thoughts, and the evolving masterpiece that is your unique self.

## Afterthoughts...

Upon the edge of metaphysical realms,
Envisioned through the lens of contemplative helms.
A canvas unfolds, the Mind's sacred scroll,
Brushstrokes of feelings and thoughts take their toll.

Heartbeats, a cadence in rhythmic embrace,
Guiding the dance, an internal grace.
Hues of emotions tango with thoughts' shadow,
Chiaroscuro nuances, a living meadow.

Ever-changing canvas, in constant flow,
Reflecting life's ebb and the experiential glow.
The mind, a craft meticulous and divine,
Each sigh, a brushstroke, an emotion's sign.

Doubt, a blend of charcoal's soft hum,
Against luminescence, where dreams become one.
Joy, a burst of golden light,
Illuminating the soul, a radiant flight.

In this analytical spotlight, emotions play,
Pigments of expression, in the mind's display.
The artist, the mind, with masterful hand,
Blends a symphony of self in a vibrant land.

Traversing mental realms, winds inspire,
Carrying forgotten narratives, tales entire.
Memory-laden meadows, laughter's domain,
Mountains of ambition, passions' fiery reign.

Delve into introspective abyss profound,
Coral reefs harbour secrets, untold, unbound.
Tears, cleansing rains, nurture creativity's soil,
Every scar, a story, a unique turmoil.

Mistakes aren't flaws, intentional smudges unfold,
Redefining horizons, leading to self-discovery untold.

~

The metaphorical canvas represents the intricacies of one's inner world, painted with the brushstrokes of emotions, thoughts, and expressions. The heartbeat becomes a rhythmic cadence guiding this internal masterpiece, emotions and thoughts blending in a nuanced chiaroscuro that mirrors the ebb and flow of experiences. The mind, portrayed as a meticulous artist, crafts subtle brushstrokes with every sigh, blending doubt and joy into a coherent symphony of self-expression.

Traversing this mental landscape, inspiration becomes a wind carrying forgotten narratives, and memory-laden meadows showcase the blossoming of laughter and the scaling of mountains of ambition. Introspection dives into fathomless depths, unveiling secrets in the coral reefs of the subconscious, where tears nurture creativity and scars tell unique stories, turning mistakes into intentional smudges that redefine the horizon of self-discovery.

## Understanding the Palette: Symphony of Samsara

*Human Senses: A Symphony of Perception*

Embark on a profound exploration of the symphony of human senses, where each note plays a crucial role in shaping the melody of our existence. Our senses—sight, hearing, touch, taste, and smell—are the skilled musicians orchestrating the vibrant tapestry of our experiences. Like masterful brushstrokes, they paint vivid landscapes in our minds, creating a narrative that resonates with laughter's echoes, the harmonies of connection, and the nuanced textures of our shared reality.

*Emotions: The Palette of the Soul*

Emotions stand as the vibrant palette that colors our perception in life's grand gallery. From the fiery reds of love's passion to the serene blues of contentment, emotions are the brushstrokes that delineate the contours of our inner world. This section delves into the intricate details of emotional landscapes, exploring their origins, expressions, and the profound influence they wield on the canvas of our lives. Emotions are the raw and authentic responses that enrich our human experience, providing depth and dimension to the stories we tell ourselves.

*Feelings: Whispers in the Silence*

Beyond the bold strokes of emotions, feelings emerge as delicate whispers in the silence of our minds. This section unravels the nuanced tapestry of sensations—the gentle comfort of belonging, the bittersweet pang of nostalgia, the ephemeral spark of curiosity. Feelings are the subtle threads that interweave through the fabric of our consciousness, offering depth and nuance to our understanding of self and others. They are the nuanced responses that add layers of complexity to the emotional landscape.

*Moods: The Atmosphere of Being*

Moods, like the ever-shifting colors of the sky, create the atmosphere of our existence. This section explores the transient nature of moods—the stormy clouds of frustration, the clear skies of happiness, and the ever-changing weather patterns that influence our daily symphony. Understanding the ebb and flow of moods enhances our awareness of the emotional landscapes we traverse. Moods are the dynamic and fluid states that shape our overall emotional climate, influencing our perception of the world around us.

*Sentiments: Echoes of the Heart*

In the labyrinth of human experience, sentiments resonate as echoes of the heart. This section unveils the enduring impressions left by experiences—the warmth of cherished memories, the cool breeze of indifference, and the echoes of meaningful connections. Sentiments, like timeless melodies, linger in the corridors of our souls, shaping our narratives with lasting impact. Sentiments are the lasting imprints that emotions and experiences leave on our hearts, influencing our perspectives and attitudes.

*Expressions: The Language of the Soul*

Expressions are the eloquent phrases and gestures that articulate the symphony within. This section examines the diverse languages through which we convey our inner world—facial expressions, body language, and the spoken word. Every expression becomes a note in the composition of our collective human symphony. Expressions are the outward manifestations of our inner states, allowing us to communicate and connect with others on a profound level.

*Passions and Affections: Fires and Ties*

Passions and affections are the roaring fires and gentle ties that bind us to our pursuits and each other. This section explores the fervent flames of ambition, the warm embraces of affection, and the intricate dance between what drives us and what connects us to the broader human experience. Passions are the intense and compelling forces that drive us towards our goals, while affections are the warm and tender bonds that connect us to others and create a sense of belonging. Together, they form the dynamic forces that shape our individual and collective journeys.

~

*Regeneration: The Evergreen Spirit*

As seasons change, so too does the human spirit possess an innate capacity for regeneration. This section delves into the resilient aspects of our being—the ability to heal from wounds, glean wisdom from challenges, and emerge with newfound strength. Just as nature rejuvenates itself, the human spirit regenerates, evergreen in its pursuit of growth, resilience, and renewal.

## The Science of Senses

Where photons dance, a ballet on your skin,
Sun's fiery brushstroke paints a summer grin.
Tongue, a canvas for the chemist's art,
Salt and sorrow, mingling from the heart.

Ears, seashells cupping ocean's symphony,
Neurons ignite, in each vibrating string.
Each scent, a molecule's whispered rhyme,
Unfurling memories, like tendrils climbing time.

Touch, a whisper on the quantum shore,
Atoms brush, a secrets' coded lore.
Eyes, telescopes on starlight's vast expanse,
Unveiling galaxies, in each tear's dim trance.

Brain, a conductor, where senses coalesce,
A concerto crafted, of joy and distress.
From whispers, thunder, a symphony composed,
Our inner landscape, vibrantly exposed.

So let the muses play, their instruments refined,
Unmute the senses, let the poem unwind.
For in this tapestry, woven fine and grand,
We hold the universe, cradled in our hand.

~

## A Boundless Wisdom: Whispers in Clay and Song

Sunlight paints the world in vibrant hues,
Each scent a memory, whispered tales infuse.
Taste, a symphony on the tongue's soft stage,
An echo of desire in every heart's cage.

Emotions bloom, like blossoms from the marsh,
Love's fiery glow, against anger's chilling harsh.
Serene moonlight on a tranquil, peaceful brow,
Fear's serpent coils, where courage takes its vow.

Moods shift like chimes in a playful, windswept tune,
Joy's vibrant tapestry, anger's bitter swoon.
Blindness veils, where doubts like shadows creep,
Resolution's light, where righteousness dares leap.

Sentiments linger, like footprints in the sand,
A yearning ache, a longing for a hand.
Strength unbound, a warrior's defiant stand,
Echoes of betrayal, etched in burning brand.

Eyes speak unspoken truths in graceful, silent sway,
Gestures of longing etched upon the clay.
A cosmic dance in every breath we hold,
Expressions whisper, stories yet untold.

Passion's fire, an arrow's swift, unerring flight,
Devotion's bond, a beacon burning bright.
Unwavering love, a warrior's oath unfurled,
Humanity's symphony, by mortal hands unfurled.

Renewal flows, like rivers to the sea,
Wounds heal like lotus, bathed in sun's decree.
In whispers shared and stories passed along,
A boundless wisdom, in every whispered song..~

## A Boundless Wisdom: Whispers in Clay and Song

A poetic narrative where virtues entwine with timeless tales, forming a profound tapestry of human experience. Seen through the lens of illumined eyes, the world unfolds, every sensory encounter a melodious whisper resonating with ancient truths.

Sunlight paints our world in shimmering hues, each scent a whispered memory, each taste a melody on the tongue's soft stage. Emotions unfold like vibrant blooms, love's fiery glow juxtaposed against anger's chilling touch. Moonlight bathes serene brows, while fear's serpent coils writhe where courage takes its stand.

Moods shift like windswept chimes, joy weaving vibrant tapestries before dissolving into anger's bitter swoon. Doubts veil like shadows, yet resolve's light bursts forth, righteousness leaping over hesitation. Sentiments linger like footprints in the sand, yearnings etched in yearning and defiance etched in a warrior's stance.

Eyes speak unspoken truths in graceful silence, gestures of longing imprinted on skin and clay. Every breath holds a cosmic dance, expressions whispering narratives yet to be voiced. Passion burns like an arrow's unerring flight, devotion a beacon guiding through darkness. Unwavering love unfurls like a warrior's oath, a testament to the human symphony played by mortal hands.

Renewal flows like rivers to the embrace of the sea, wounds healing like lotus blossoms kissed by the sun. In whispered stories and shared experiences, boundless wisdom resides, sung in every beating heart. We are but notes in a grand composition, our emotions weaving a tapestry of shared humanity.

Thus, we dance, laugh, and weep, a swirling storm of light and shadow, forever bound by the whispers of the soul. In this tapestry of emotions, lies the essence of our being, a testament to the vibrant complexity of being human.

The composition culminates with an invitation to partake in the divine symphony, where senses, emotions, and souls converge. Within the vast expanse of Vedas and myths, hands unite in boundless knowledge bathed in divine illumination. The verses exalt the profound interconnection between human experiences and the timeless virtues embedded in cultural myths and legends.

~

## Human Senses

Our senses, the **Five weavers** muses of this boundless canvas, paint with an infinite palette. The sun-kissed heat of a summer day on your skin, the bittersweet tang of tears on your tongue, the thunderous roar of a symphony in your ears, all these are the threads that weave the tapestry of your perception. Each taste, each scent, each tingle is a whispered verse in your poet's ear, a secret language waiting to be unravelled....

Our senses, the mischievous muses of this boundless canvas, dance with an infinite palette, painting our reality in strokes of sun-kissed fire and moonlit whispers. The summer's caress lingers on bare skin, a memory of warmth on canvas. Bittersweet tears, their tang on the tongue, leave salty brushstrokes of loss and relief. The thunderous poem of a symphony, drums pounding rhythm onto bone, vibrates across the canvas, a visceral echo.

Each whisper of taste, a haiku on the tongue, each sigh of scent, a poem in the air, every tingle, a secret code tapped on the skin – these are the whispered verses in our poet's ear, a language etched in sensation, waiting to be unravelled. They are the raw materials of our perception, the threads woven into the tapestry of who we are.

Close your eyes, and feel the world bloom on your skin. The cool caress of rain, the prickling heat of firelight, the gentle dance of breeze against your cheek like each a brushstroke on your inner canvas, painting landscapes of experience. Let the symphony of sound flood you, the birdsong's concerto, the murmur of wind in leaves, the rhythmic thrum of your own heartbeat for each note a verse whispering its story.

Open your eyes, and see the world burst into colour. The fiery hues of a sunset, the emerald whispers of a forest, the sapphire secrets of the ocean each a glimpse into another dimension, a brushstroke layering your perception. Let the fragrance of freshly baked bread, the salty sting of the sea, the earthy kiss of damp soil like scent a language of memory, a brushstroke weaving the tapestry of your past.

For in this grand dance of the senses, no experience is lost, no detail too small. They are the whispers of the muse, the brushstrokes of the artist, the verses of the poet, forever shaping, reshaping, and enriching the magnificent tapestry of our being. So let us listen, let us feel, let us see, and allow the boundless symphony of sensation to paint our own unique masterpiece, a story whispered in a thousand vibrant tongues.

## Five Weavers: Weaving the Mind's Masterpiece

Five weavers bold, on the cosmic loom,
Paint landscapes in the mind's vast room.

Sight, a sunlit brushstroke on life's canvas,
Recalls golden days and moments amass.
A splash of blue in the sea's rhythmic swell,
Lost laughter echoes, a tale to tell.

Hearing, a storyteller in the unseen,
Moonbeams sing lullabies, joyous and serene.
Laughter's cascade, a melody sublime,
Tears' soft drip, a mournful, rhythmic rhyme.

Touch, a mother's hand, gentle and kind,
Moulds memories in the sands of the mind.
Lover's brush, a feather's tender sigh,
Forges bonds beneath the vast sky.

Taste, a chef with fire's passionate kiss,
Spices joy heals the grief abyss.
Sweet honeyed lips or a stolen bite,
Sour stings, lost appetite's fight.

Smell, a perfumer's magical art,
Embodies memories close to the heart.
Cinnamon dreams and childhood's gleam,
Salty spray, a windswept, wild scream.

Thus, painted worlds, each vibrant hue,
The symphony of senses, always true.
Fine brushstrokes weave, blend, and bend,
The Canvas of the Mind, a tale without an end.

~

## Senses as Inspiration

Let the world be your muse. The wind whispering secrets through ancient trees, the rain drumming a lullaby on rooftops, the scent of freshly baked bread warming the air, all these are the voices that call to your soul. Immerse yourself in the symphony of the senses, let them spark your imagination, ignite your brushstrokes. Every sight, every sound, every scent is a verse waiting to be written and read forever..

Let the world be your muse, as a canvas vast,
Where whispers of wind paint secrets to last...
On ancient forts, where sunlight weaves,
A verdant ode, like meadows rustling leaves.

Rain's drumming rhythm, singing a lullaby,
on roof drumming, dancing, tears of the sky...
Of comfort shared, and laughter's chime,
A bond of home, beyond the tales of time...

Open your eyes, see the colors do sing,
nature's way of daily vibrant offering...
few flowers bloom, beside the wild stream,
A whispering the verses and knitting a dream...

Taste the rain, like a kiss so serene,
Feel the sun's caress, on weathered skin...
Every breath is a promise, as a lasting bold,
on the canvas of your heart, as tales unfold...

Let our passion's fire ignite such a scene,
With every sight, and whatever we have seen...
Do dance with life, in all vibrant hues,
When senses get alive, as inspiration imbues...

For in each soul, each scent, each touch,
A masterpiece awaits, waiting to be clutched...

# Emotions

Ah, emotions! The fiery brushstrokes of anger, the gentle blues of contentment, the emerald tendrils of jealousy that twist around the heart, the golden joy that explodes like a supernova. These are the tempests and sunrises of our inner landscape, shaping the contours of every thought and action. Learn their language, the tremor in your voice, the clench of your jaw, the sparkle in your eyes. Each ripple of emotion is a stanza in your epic poem, a hidden rhyme waiting to be unearthed.

## Whispers of the Soul: A Symphony in Hues

A palette vast, held within the soul,
Cause feelings flare, and stories stroll.
Then tranquil blues, contentment's sigh,
As summer skies paint that vibrant sky,

A gentle brush, a whispered word,
Serene waves serenely so stirred.
A bitter tang, a poisoned well,
Secret whispers, that stories tell.

Golden bursts, were Laughter's song,
Hopes reborn when happiness throng
Tempests rage, when tempers rise,
Sadden hue of a heartfelt dis-guise,

The canvas shifts, with fleeting breath,
A symphony of soul, in life and death.
Learn the language, whispered low,
Tremble of voice, and teardrop's flow,

Unravel stanzas, in the lost beat of rhyme,
Unearthing tales of keen within your time...

~

## The Language of Emotions: Our Inner Storms

While emotions paint in fiery hues,
Linger whispers, soft and subtle clues.
Not grand pronouncements, bold and bright,
But gentle brushstrokes, bathed in light.

The comfort hush of belonging's touch,
A feather's sigh, a loved one's clutch.
Warm embers glow where roots entwined,
A silent symphony, defined.

Nostalgia's sting, a honeyed tear,
Golden memories, bittersweet and near.
Sunsets whispered, moments flown,
Echoes linger, seeds are sown.

Curiosity's spark, a playful flame,
Dancing embers, whispering a name.
Uncharted paths, a question's call,
The veil lifts, shadows start to fall.

Embrace these whispers, subtle threads,
Woven tapestries where comfort spreads.
In fleeting moments, truth takes flight,
The tapestry of self, bathed in gentle light.

For in these nuances, softly sung,
The symphony of being is unstrung.
Beyond the bold, beyond the loud,
The whispers tell where beauties found.

So listen close, let senses guide,
In hushed whispers, truth will reside.
The tapestry of self, forever spun,
With every feeling, under the unseen sun.

# Unveiling Those 32 Shades of Emotions

Imagine from a point of view of as a poet, brush poised above a canvas vast as the human experience. But this canvas isn't crafted from mundane linen; it's woven from the very fabric of our emotions, a luminous tapestry pulsing with 32 distinct hues. First, the sun-kissed yellows of joy and amusement dance across the surface, laughter echoing like wind chimes in a summer breeze. Contentment paints its gentle blues, whispering serenity like the sigh of a moonlit wave. Then come the vibrant oranges of excitement and enthusiasm, brushstrokes fuelled by passion's embers, chasing horizons with fearless abandon.

But the canvas isn't solely bathed in golden light. Shades of storm arise – the fiery reds of anger, the icy blues of fear, the shadowed purples of grief and sorrow. The poet doesn't shy away from these hues, for they too are threads in the intricate tapestry of humanity. The raw bite of disgust, the gnawing ache of loneliness, the venomous green of envy – each evokes a visceral response, a testament to the depth and complexity of our emotional landscape. Yet, even amidst the shadows, flickers of resilience spark. Gratitude paints its sun-dappled greens, offering solace and anchoring the soul. Acceptance, a silvered grey, weaves itself into the fabric, softening the blows of disappointment and loss. And curiosity, a playful gold, guides the poet's hand, forever seeking new pathways through the labyrinth of experience.

This is the symphony, a composition played on the strings of our shared humanity. Each brushstroke, each shade, a testament to the richness of our inner lives, the constant interplay of light and shadow, joy and sorrow, laughter and tears. And in the poet's hand, these emotions become not burdens, but pigments, transforming the mundane into masterpiece, the fleeting into eternal.

## Sun-Kissed Strokes: The Dance of Positive Emotions

The tapestry unfurls, bathed in the golden light of joy. Laughter spills like cascading sunlight, echoing in tinkling bells and wind-chimes of amusement. Contentment hums a lullaby, waves caressing the shores of serenity with gentle whispers. Excitement paints the horizon with fiery oranges, hearts drumming a rhythm of anticipation, while enthusiasm's torch flames high, casting shadows of daring and ambition.

Gratitude's verdant tendrils reach towards the sun, twining around every blessing, big and small. Hope's whisper dances on the breeze, a seed blossoming into possibilities. Interest, a boundless wellspring, draws the soul towards wonder, while love's tapestry, woven from shared laughter and whispered secrets, paints the canvas with radiant hues.

Pride, a soaring eagle, lifts its wings on victories earned, while satisfaction sighs with the quiet contentment of a journey well-travelled. Awe stands spellbound beneath the canopy of stars, its brushstrokes tracing the grandeur of existence. Inspiration ignites, a spark leaping from the embers of experience, setting alight new paths of creation.

~

## Joy, Amusement and Contentment

Sun-kissed laughter, a windblown chime,
Joy ignites, a golden rhyme.
Heart a drum, feet a dancing flame,
World aglow, whispered by no name.

Toddler smiles, eyes alight with glee,
Amusement's spark, setting spirits free.
Tongue-tied giggles, a playful chase,
Joy unfurled, in an open space.

Warm embers glow, contentment's sigh,
Sunlight slumbers, clouds drift by.
Hushed content, a gentle stream,
Peaceful whispers, whispered dream.

Barefoot steps on wet velvet grass,
Sun-warmed skin, moments that surpass.
Birdsong symphony, leaves alight,
Joy's gentle echo, bathed in gentle light.

Whispers of wind through summer trees,
Swaying branches, rustling ease.
Contentment's hand, a lullaby,
Clouds adrift in an endless sky.

Honeyed laughter, shared delight,
Sun-kissed faces, bathed in gentle light.
Joy's embrace, a whispered rhyme,
Human experience, in its purest prime.

~

## Excitement, Enthusiasm, and Interest

Sparks ignite, a restless thrill,
Excitement whispers, standing still?
No, feet a blur, a pulse that drums,
Chasing horizons, chasing suns.

Enthusiasm's torch, a flaming brand,
Leap of faith, across the shifting sand.
Eyes ablaze, a fearless soul,
Painting dreams upon a boundless scroll.

Curiosity's flame, a flickering spark,
Unravelling secrets, leaving its mark.
Whispers of wonder, voices untold,
A tapestry woven, brave and bold.

Heartbeat quickens, breath held tight,
Excitement paints the coming night.
Stars as compass, shadows dance,
In every journey, second chance.

Enthusiasm's roar, a lion's call,
Conquering mountains, standing tall.
No path untrodden, no wall too high,
The fire within, reaching for the sky.

Curiosity's whispers, secrets heard,
Unlocking treasures, every spoken word.
Worlds within worlds, stories untold,
An endless quest, forever bold.

So let the embers paint the dawn,
Embrace the thrill, till life is gone.
Excitement's pulse, a guiding light,
Enthusiasm's fire, burning ever bright.

~

## Hope, Love, Gratitude

Where embers flicker, hope takes flight,
A silver thread in starlit night.
A whispered promise, soft and strong,
That dawn will break, however long.

Love, a crimson bloom, unfurls,
In tender touch, in whispered words.
A tapestry of hearts entwined,
In shared laughter, spirits aligned.

Gratitude, a moonlit stream,
Flows gentle, a calming dream.
For sunlit days and whispered grace,
For every breath, a loving space.

Hope, a fragile butterfly,
On wings of dawn, it seeks the sky.
Aching wounds begin to mend,
With every sunrise, hope transcends.

Love, a fire in the winter's hold,
Warming souls, both young and old.
In sheltering arms, in tear-filled eyes,
A boundless strength, that never dies.

Gratitude, a whispered sigh,
For every star that lights the sky.
For simple joys, for laughter's chime,
For every moment, fleeting, sublime.

With grateful hearts, let spirits soar,
In every breath, forevermore.
For in these threads, so brightly spun,
The symphony of life has begun.

~

## Pride, Satisfaction, Serenity

Sun-kissed peak, or a summit won,
Pride unfurls, a crimson spun.
Effort's echo, sweat-sweet air,
Triumph's banner hoisted there.

Wings unfurled, a spirit free,
Pride soars high, where mountains be.
Echoes of praise, a distant bell,
Worthy deeds, the story tell.

Golden sigh, a battle fought,
Satisfaction whispers softly caught.
Rest's embrace, a weary smile,
Journey's end, so much worthwhile

Honeyed breath, a moment held,
Satisfaction's peace, in stories spelled.
No regrets, no shadows cast,
Just sunlit paths forever passed.

Moonlit lake, a mind at ease,
Serenity whispers through the peace.
Silence sings, a gentle rhyme,
Tranquil space, beyond all time.

Starlit gaze, a heart set free,
Serenity's hush, beneath the tree.
Waves of calm, on quiet shores,
Peaceful whispers, evermore.

Savour the rest, with grateful sigh,
Satisfaction's whispers, never die.
Serenity's touch, a whispered song,
Where worries fade, and we belong.

~

## Awe and Inspiration

Beneath a canvas vast, where stars ignite,
Awe whispers secrets, bathed in silvered light.
valleys yawn, oceans cradle the moonlit flame,
Cosmic brushstrokes etch a whispered name.

Inspiration's ember, kindled from above,
A brushstroke dances, guided by pure love.
Melodies unheard, poems yet unsung,
Whispers of creation, on a vibrant tongue.

Galaxies swirl, a cosmic ballet's grace,
Awestruck silence, in time and endless space.
A mountain's breath, a whispered lullaby,
Eternity's echo, beneath a boundless sky.

Inspiration's hand, on canvas bare,
Unveils a masterpiece, a beauty to share.
From whispered wonders to symphonies untold,
Humanity's story, in vibrant hues unfolds.

So let us wander, beneath the cosmic dome,
Embrace the awe, let wonder find its home.
With hearts receptive, let inspiration spark,
And paint our lives, with beauty's vibrant arc.

For in these whispers, where awe and light combine,
The human spirit, forever divine.
A symphony of wonder, ever sung,
Were awe and inspiration, forever young.

~

## Shadowed Threads: The Symphony of Negative Emotions

The brush dips into a deeper well, and the tapestry takes a turn. Anger's crimson scorch marks its territory, a storm cloud rumbling on the horizon of serenity. Anxiety's cold tendrils weave a net of worry, casting doubt in shimmering threads, while boredom's stagnant fog descends, a leaden weight upon the spirit.

Contempt's icy sneer twists lips into frozen daggers, pushing boundaries with silent judgment. Disgust recoils, the face contorted with aversion, a shield against the ugliness of the world. Fear, a primal dance between fight and flight, takes hold in the face of the unknown.

Frustration knots the threads, a tangled mess that unravels only with lessons learned. Guilt's heavy cloak weighs upon the soul, seeking solace in the gentle wind of forgiveness. Sadness' raindrops fall, each tear a whispered memory, a testament to love lost and dreams deferred. Shame's crimson blush burns beneath the skin, a secret yearning for acceptance in the eyes of another.

## Rage Unleashed

In the depths of the soul, a tempest brews,
Anger's storm rages, fierce and true.
Reason melts in the forge, a searing ire,
As the spirit resides in the blaze's fire.

A lightning strike heralds an infernal birth,
Consuming all, this tempest of wrath.
Thunderous echoes, the earthquakes,
Silence shattered as anger overtakes.

But in this fiery inferno, a lesson is learned,
Anger, a blaze that leaves hearts burned.
Amidst its searing dance, a choice takes flight,
Tame the flames or succumb to their might.

~

"Rage Unleashed" vividly captures the tumultuous nature of anger and its impact on the soul. The context begins by describing the depths of the soul as a brewing tempest, emphasizing the fierce and genuine nature of the rage that surfaces. Reason is depicted as melting in the forge of this searing ire, and the spirit is portrayed as residing in the intense fire of the blaze.

A metaphorical lightning strike heralds the birth of this infernal tempest, consuming everything in its path. The poem employs powerful imagery such as thunderous echoes and earthquakes to convey the overwhelming force of anger, shattering the silence as it overtakes.

However, amidst the fiery inferno suggests that there is a lesson to be learned. Anger is characterized as a blaze that can leave hearts burned, emphasizing its destructive potential. The concluding lines introduce a crucial choice; whether to tame the flames or succumb to their might, adding a layer of reflection and agency in the face of anger's intensity.

## Whispers of Restlessness

Amidst the midnight's hush, anxiety stirs,
Its whispers persistent, a haunting that recurs.
A symphony of unease, a ceaseless stream,
Through dreams it weaves, an unsettling seam.

Restless thoughts hold the mind in chains,
Lost in worry's labyrinth, where unease reigns.
A heartbeat's drum, an anxious rhyme,
A dance with shadows in the corridors of time.

But within anxiety's clutch and its demand,
Emerges a strength, a will to withstand.
To navigate the maze, seek a calming shore,
In the sea of unrest, find a tranquil core.

~

"Whispers of Restlessness" paints a vivid picture of the persistent and haunting nature of anxiety. The context begins by setting the scene in the midnight hush, where anxiety stirs, and its whispers become an unsettling symphony that recurs. The imagery of a ceaseless stream and the weaving of unease through dreams evoke a sense of restlessness that pervades the mind. Restless thoughts are described as holding the mind in chains, creating a labyrinth of worry where unease reigns supreme. The heartbeat's drum and the anxious rhyme contribute to the portrayal of anxiety as a dance with shadows in the corridors of time, emphasizing its pervasive influence.

Despite anxiety's clutch, the poem introduces a hopeful note. Within the demands of anxiety, a strength emerges as a will to withstand. The imagery of navigating a maze and seeking a calming shore in the sea of unrest conveys the idea of finding resilience and tranquillity at the core, offering a glimpse of overcoming the restlessness.

## Dull Echoes

Boredom, a subtle and insidious foe,
Creeping softly, casting a listless shadow.
The clock ticks in a monotonous tune,
As boredom settles beneath the languid moon.

A yawn escapes, a sigh softly plays,
Boredom's haze in the mind's intricate maze.
In the void of shine, creativity sparks,
A dormant flame in the diminishing dark.

Yet, boredom's canvas, a blank slate,
A challenge to innovate, to create.
In the dull echoes, find a hidden thrill,
Boredom's whispers, an invitation to skill.

~

"Dull Echoes" captures the essence of boredom as a subtle and insidious force that casts a listless shadow. The context opens with boredom described as a creeping foe, softly making its presence felt, while the clock's monotonous ticking reinforces the dull atmosphere. The use of "languid moon" adds to the sense of a slow and uneventful passage of time.

Expressions of boredom, such as a yawn and a sigh, are depicted, emphasizing the mind's intricate maze affected by boredom's haze. However, the thought takes a turn by highlighting the potential for creativity to spark in the void left by boredom. The dormant flame in the diminishing dark suggests that boredom might inadvertently lead to the emergence of creative thoughts and ideas. Then concludes by portraying boredom's canvas as a blank slate, challenging individuals to innovate and create. In the dull echoes of boredom, there's a hidden thrill, and boredom's whispers become an invitation to skilfully engage with the challenges it presents.

## Contempt, Disgust, Guilt

A cold wind whispers, where contempt takes flight,
Iced fingers curl, around a heart of blight.
Twisted lips, a sneer's disdainful line,
Where shadows dance, and virtues intertwine.

Bitter bile churns, a serpent's coiled embrace,
Disgust’s green gaze stains every smiling face.
Beauty curdles, to a rancid smear,
The world recoils, in fetid atmosphere.

Guilt's leaden weight, a crushing, silent stone,
Breathless whispers, of deeds you've made your own.
Memories sting, like phantom lashes' bite,
Haunted echoes, through the lonely night.

But wait, dear soul, where shadows twist and turn,
A spark may flicker, a lesson yet to learn.
Confront the ice, thaw the frozen core,
Let empathy's hand, crack open sorrow's door.

Against the serpent, raise a cleansing tide,
Let kindness bloom, where disgust had tried.
Embrace forgiveness, a balm for wounds unseen,
Guilt's heavy cloak, a chrysalis, not spleen.

From frozen landscapes, let new growth unfold,
Where shadows cower, in stories yet untold.
For in the depths, where darkness takes its stand,
Compassion’s light can rewrite the land.

Do breathe again, let shadows slowly fade,
In empathy's embrace, a future unafraid.
For even thorns, can yield a fragrant bloom,
And darkness holds, the promise of a moon.

## Fear, Frustration and Sadness

Where shadows cling, and whispers turn to dread,
Fear's icy fingers trace a path unsaid.
The heart a drum, in frantic, trembling beat,
A caged bird's wings, against the bars retreat.

Frustration's knot, a tangled thread of toil,
Muscles clenched tight, against unyielding soil.
Hope's embers dim, beneath the ashes grey,
Will dawns ignite, or shadows hold their sway?

Sadness, a storm cloud, gathers in the soul,
Tears, gentle rain, where dreams have lost their goal.
Memories echo, in a mournful sigh,
The weight of longing, in a tearful eye.

But hold, dear heart, in darkness, stars unseen,
Can guide the way, where shadows intervene.
Embrace the fear, a compass in the night,
To navigate the path, towards new sunlight.

Unravel frustration, unwind the tangled thread,
Let patience bloom, where shadows once misled.
For every knot, holds strength within its core,
A Phoenix waits, reborn forevermore.

And in the hush, where sadness finds its voice,
Let gentle whispers, make a joyful choice.
For mourning's rain, nurtures the fertile ground,
Where seeds of hope, in silent tears, are found.

Just walk on, through the shadowed wood,
With fear as lantern, frustration understood.
Embrace the rain, let sadness have its say,
For in the darkness, dawn will break today.

## Shame, Sorrow, and Loneliness

In whispers low, where shadows drape and cling,
Shame's poisoned thorns, their barbed whispers sing.
A crimson blush, a shrinking inward gaze,
A hidden self, lost in a self-made maze.

Sorrow's tide, a crashing, mournful wave,
Washes over shores, where joy once clave.
Empty rooms echo with a hollow moan,
A lonely wind, through memories unknown.

Loneliness, a shroud that chills the bone,
A hollow echo, where connections flown.
A silent scream, unheard in the vast night,
Yearning for warmth, in the dim, flickering light.

But hold, dear soul, beneath the thorns' cruel sting,
A seed of strength, where healing wings can spring.
Confront the shame, its whispers face and quell,
Embrace forgiveness, let the shackles melt.

Let tears cleanse the soul, as the sun breaks through,
New landscapes bloom, where once despair grew.
And in the hush, where loneliness takes hold,
Reach out, dear heart, let your story unfold.

For bonds unseen, like threads in the moon's light,
Connect us all, in darkness of the night.
For shame's release, sorrow's cleansing rain,
And loneliness' embrace, all heal the pain.

Step out, dear soul, where shadows start to fade,
In shared connections, a haven is made.
For in the weaving of hearts, hand in hand,
We find our strength, in this human land.

## Envy, Grief, Jealousy

A bitter vine, envy twists and climbs,
Strangling joy in shadows, stealing sunshine times.
Another's fortune, a poisoned, tempting fruit,
Leaving your own garden barren, parched, and mute.

Jealousy's barbed wire, a twisting, burning crown,
Crowding out dreams, dragging hopes down.
Comparison's serpent, whispering in your ear,
Dimming your own fire, feeding doubt and fear.

Grief, a raven's wing, shrouding the sunlit sky,
Where laughter danced, now tears unbidden lie.
Echoes of laughter, like ghosts in empty halls,
Haunted by a love that used to stand so tall.

But wait, dear heart, in envy's bitter vine,
Lies hidden wisdom, a potent, healing wine.
Turn its tendrils green to tendrils strong and wise,
Nurture your own orchard, where vibrant beauty lies.

Unravel jealousy's tight-fisted coil,
Let your palms unfurl, embrace your own unique spoil.
Celebrate the sunlight in another's eyes,
Let your own star rise, claim your own clear skies.

And in the hush, where grief's raven takes its flight,
Let tears be rain, to nourish inner light.
Memories, stained glass, casting colourful rays,
A kaleidoscope of love, through grief's misty haze.

So rise above, where envy's vines would bind,
Release the grip, where jealousy would blind.
With the open minds and hearts that give,
We rise, transformed, in this resilient weave.

## Surprise, Rejection and Vulnerability

A gasp escapes, where expectation sleeps,
Surprise awakens, where reality leaps.
The world rewrites, in colors unforeseen,
A canvas flipped, where shadows once had been.

Rejection's sting, a serpent at the gate,
Whispering whispers, sealing hope's debate.
Door's slam shut, on dreams once held so dear,
Echoes of "no" pierce through the waiting ear.

Vulnerability, a whisper on the breeze,
Barefoot heart, adrift on stormy seas.
Exposed and raw, where walls used to reside,
A trembling trust, laid open to the tide.

But hold, dear soul when surprise rearranges,
Embrace the chaos, see rhythms play the changes.
Unlearn the script, rewrite with curious hand,
Discover treasures, in this shifting sand.

Rejection's wound, though sharp, will scar and heal,
Strength blooms anew, where thorns no longer feel.
Let go of doors, build open, boundless skies,
Where wings unfurl, and dreams take flight and rise.

Vulnerability, a tender, blossoming rose,
In open hearts, true connection grows.
Let tears be rain, to nourish fertile ground,
Where trust takes root, in love deeply profound.

Embrace the raw, the tender, and the free,
For in vulnerability, strength you truly see.
Surprise, rejection, vulnerability's embrace,
Forge resilience, in this human landscape's space.

## Threads of Neutrality: The Canvas of Reflection

But the human tapestry is not merely woven from light and shadow. Neutrality holds its own space, a canvas upon which reflection dances. Acceptance's silver threads weave through the narrative, a constant hum of understanding beneath the vibrant storm of emotions.

Curiosity's playful fingers trace uncharted corners, forever seeking new stories to write. Disappointment's sting becomes a brushstroke of learning, a catalyst for growth. Neutrality, a blank space within the whirlwind, offers a pause for recalibration, a moment to breathe before the next stroke.

Relief washes over, a cleansing wave as the story unfolds. Surprise, a jolt, throws open the doors of perception, revealing new pathways in the blink of an eye. Each thread, every emotion, every stroke, a testament to the richness, complexity, and sheer awe-inspiring beauty of the human experience.

## Acceptance, Disappointment & Neutrality

Acceptance, a beacon in the tempest's flight,
Guiding hope's flicker through the darkest night.
Within its calm, shattered hearts find reprieve,
Embraced by solace when the healings arrive.

Disappointment, a chalice, bitter and deep,
Yet wisdom's elixir, waiting in its sleep.
Though sails may droop, and winds may veer,
Strength blossoms in lessons, crystal clear.

Neutrality, life's fulcrum, poised and serene,
Balancing on the axis, emotions in between.
Unmoved by tides of joy or sorrow's sting,
A tranquil anchor, where the soul takes wing.

Acceptance, a whispered vow, sincere and true,
A haven for vulnerability to renew.
Echoes of loss may linger like the tide,
Yet Acceptance's current reshapes where tears once cried.

Disappointment, a master, sharp and keen,
Etching shadows, where lessons are gleaned.
Thorns transformed, bearing wisdom's tender bloom,
Resilience rising from the shadowed tomb.

Neutrality, the compass in the soul's grand play,
Guiding through currents, emotions in array.
A vast canvas, serene and unmarred,
Where whispers of wisdom, untethered, are charred.

Acceptance, Disappointment, Neutrality's blend,
In life's tapestry, harmonious threads ascend.
Woven together, a vibrant tableau unfolds,
The human tale, a masterpiece in stories untold.

## Curiosity, Relief & Surprise

Curiosity, a spark, a kitten's paw,
Unwinding secrets, chipping at lives raw.
Through cracks in knowledge, it peeks and pries,
A lantern raised to where the unknown lies.

Relief, a sigh, a tension gently shed,
The burden when lifted; fears fled.
Like rain on parched earth, it cools the soul,
Washing away worries, making one whole.

Surprise, a jolt, a firework in the night,
Disrupting patterns with its sudden light.
The script reshuffled, expectations tossed,
In the upheaval, a new world almost crossed.

But wait, dear heart, where curiosity spins,
Embrace the journey, the questions within.
Let knowledge bloom, a mind ever wild,
Where wonder wanders, like a curious child.

Relief's exhale, a breath for renewal's sake,
A pause, a reset, before the leap you take.
Cherish the quiet, the solace hard-won,
For strength recharges beneath the setting sun.

And in surprise, where chaos paints the sky,
A chance to dance, to laugh, to touch the sky.
Embrace the unexpected, the twists and turns,
For in their wake, adventure brightly burns.

So let curiosity's flame forever spark,
Relief's soft whispers soothe the weary dark.
And in surprise, find joy in life's grand stage,
Where every moment turns a vibrant page.

# Feelings

In the intricate landscape of human experience, the interplay between feelings and emotions unfolds as a captivating narrative, each with its distinct nuances and hues. While the terms "feelings" and "emotions" are often used interchangeably, a closer examination reveals subtle distinctions that contribute to the complex richness of our inner lives.

Feelings, akin to the delicate brushstrokes on a canvas, are the nuanced, subjective responses to emotions. They are the individualized, personal interpretations of emotional states, offering a more refined and introspective dimension to the human psyche. Unlike emotions, which are often considered more immediate and instinctual responses to external stimuli, feelings linger and weave themselves into the fabric of our inner world, shaping our perspectives and colouring our thoughts.

Emotions, on the other hand, are the primal, instinctive reactions to stimuli that surge through us, often evoking physiological responses. Joy, fear, anger, and sadness are archetypal emotions, universally recognized across cultures. Emotions are the vivid strokes of color that paint the broader strokes on the canvas of our consciousness. They are spontaneous, powerful, and serve as the foundation upon which feelings build their intricate tapestry.

While emotions are somewhat universal and shared by all humans, feelings are deeply personal and influenced by individual experiences, memories, and interpretations. For instance, the emotion of joy might manifest as a feeling of contentment for one person, while another might experience it as a surge of elation. This divergence highlights the personalized nature of feelings, emphasizing the unique lens through which each individual views and processes their emotional landscape.

Navigating the complex interplay between emotions and feelings requires a nuanced understanding of oneself and others. Recognizing and articulating these subtleties can lead to increased emotional intelligence, fostering improved communication and empathy and thus embarking on a journey of self-discovery, cultivating a deeper connection with their inner selves and the shared human experience.

## Beyond Labels: The Nuances of Inner Sensations

Beyond the straightforward classifications of emotions lies a realm of intricate and nuanced experiences known as feelings. These subtle brushstrokes on the canvas of our inner world add depth and richness to the human experience.

Ultimately, this discussion underscores the idea that understanding and accepting the diverse range of feelings is integral to a holistic approach to emotional well-being. By navigating through the delicate nuances of inner sensations, individuals can cultivate a deeper connection with themselves, fostering resilience, empathy, and a more profound appreciation for the intricacies that make the human experience so beautifully complex.

Amidst the urban sprawl, the neon lights of the city have left an indelible mark on my memories like a vivid kaleidoscope where dreams eagerly pursue the concrete skies. With each sunrise, a fresh canvas unfolds, and every experience becomes a smudge of colour, contributing to the ever-evolving masterpiece of my being.

Once, faith stood as an unyielding monument, carved in stone and weathered by life's tempests. Doubt has woven itself alongside conviction, creating a context adorned with threads of older insight and hard-earned lessons, gleaming in the ever-shifting light of understanding.

My story is not confined to neat rhymed stanzas; it sprawls across the pages written in ink that bears witness to laughter and tears, sunlit hills, dense jungles, and storm-wracked trees. My journey is not a straight line but runs down the small lanes and highways unveiling hidden doorways and secret chambers within the intricate self.

## Cognitive, Diverse and Nuanced

Within the mind's labyrinthine fold,
Where tangled thoughts and memories unfold,
A symphony of whispers takes its flight,
Cognitive whispers, bathed in starlit light.

No single note, no static drone, but hues,
A kaleidoscope where logic confuses.
With intuition, dreams, a vibrant blend,
A context where reason's fail to transcend.

Diverse they dance, a swirling, shifting tide,
From abstract musings, where concepts hide,
To concrete facts, like pillars carved in stone,
Each facet gleams, a story to be known.

Nuanced they breathe, a tapestry so fine,
Where shades of doubt with certainty entwine,
Where questions bloom, like orchids in the rain,
And answers whisper, soft, against the pain.

For here, within this realm, where thoughts reside,
No single truth, no path rigidly tied,
But endless possibilities take wing,
A symphony of being, where we truly sing.

So let us wander, through this vibrant space,
Embrace the chaos, find our own sweet grace,
For in this dance of cognitive delight,
We paint the canvas of our inner light.

## Experiences, Beliefs, and Interpretations

Through woven tapestries of time we tread,
Experiences like threads, where stories spread.
Sun-drenched beaches, windswept mountain height,
Love's whispered echo, shadows of the night.

Beliefs, the loom where threads together bind,
A guiding tapestry, shaping mind and kind.
From whispered prayers to etched ancestral lore,
Anchors in the storm, when tempests roar.

Interpretations, brushes light and bright,
Dip in the well of feeling, paint with inner light.
Joy's vibrant hues, where sorrow's teardrop stains,
Each stroke unveils the world, through sunlit rains.

The threads entwine, a vibrant, living mesh,
Experiences, beliefs, interpretations thresh.
The artist stands, before the grand design,
Unveiling truths, where mortal and divine.

For life's a canvas, vast and ever-changing,
Each brushstroke, breath, a new perspective ranging.
So let your tapestry unfold, unfurled,
Experiences, beliefs, interpretations in the world.

Embrace the colors, dark and light, and true,
The tapestry of self, forever fresh and new.
With every thread, a whisper, soft and strong,
The symphony of being, where we belong.

~

# Moods

Ah, moods, the fickle winds that ruffle the curtains of our souls. One moment, we bask in the golden sunrise of joyful exuberance, laughter bubbling like champagne in the heart. The next, we huddle beneath the leaden clouds of despair, shadows clinging like damp wool. There's the playful breeze of mischief, the crackling storm of fury, the tender hush of melancholy. They weave a tapestry as vast and ever-changing as the sky itself.

But navigating this moodscape is no easy feat. Like a sailor caught in a squall, we're tossed and turned by the tides of emotion. The vibrant dance of excitement can morph into the feverish waltz of anxiety, the gentle lull of contentment into the numbing stillness of apathy. It's a constant dance, a balancing act on a tightrope strung between sunshine and shadows. Yet, within this mercurial panorama, lies the art of resilience. We learn to weather the storms, to find pockets of peace amidst the roaring winds. Just as a lone oak stands tall against the fury of the tempest, so too can we cultivate a steady core, an inner haven where serenity whispers even when the world outside howls.

Take joy, for instance. It may come like a sudden burst of fireworks, dazzling and fleeting. But its embers can be nurtured, fanned into a gentle, warming flame that lights our path even in the gloomiest nights. Let laughter be your sunrise, the memory of a shared smile a ray of sunshine on a cloudy day.

And what of sorrow, that heavy cloak we all must wear at times? It, too, has its purpose. In its quiet depths, we find resilience, a chance to mend the frayed edges of our being. Let your tears be rain, cleansing and nourishing, paving the way for new growth. For even in the aftermath of a storm, wildflowers bloom. Learn to dance with the winds, to find solace in the sun and strength in the rain. Remember, the vastness of your emotional sky is a testament to the richness of your being. Let your moods paint your canvas, each one a brushstroke in the masterpiece of your life. And in the quiet corners of your soul, cultivate the garden of peace, where you can always find your way back to the light, no matter how dark the storm may rage.

## Joy, Happiness, and Laughter

These are the brushstrokes of sunrise, painting our world in golden laughter and infectious giggles. Hummingbirds dance with joy, their iridescent feathers reflecting the vibrant melody of a life well-lived. These are the shared smiles around a crackling fire, the echoes of childhood games resonating through summer evenings, the spontaneous bursts of delight that ignite our souls like fireflies on a starry night.

*"Joy's Symphony: A Dance of Delight"*

Sunbeams brush the dew-kissed grass,
Painting joy in morning's glass.
Laughter ripples, clear and bright,
Hummingbirds dance in feathered light.

Crackling flames paint warmth and cheer,
As childhood echoes fill the year.
Games and stories, hand in hand,
Golden moments, grains of sand.

Spontaneous sparks ignite the soul,
Like fireflies that make us whole.
Belly laughs and twinkling eyes,
Joy's symphony, in bright disguise.

For life's a canvas, vast and wide,
Were joy's brushstrokes, forever glide.
Let laughter sing, and hearts take flight,
In the golden dance of pure delight.

Now raise your voice and let it soar,
Embrace the joy, forevermore.
For in this world, where shadows fall,
Joy's laughter echoes through it all.

## Excitement, Elation, and Anticipation

They're the butterflies trapped in our stomachs, fluttering wings of dreams yet to unfold. Imagine the giddy climb of a rollercoaster, the whispered promises of a journey uncharted, the adrenaline rush of stepping onto a stage bathed in spotlights. These are the whispers of "what if" that set our hearts ablaze, the seeds of adventure planted in fertile ground, the wind in our sails as we navigate towards thrilling horizons.

*"Fluttering Horizons: A Symphony of Dreams"*

Butterflies take flight in bellies deep,
A silent symphony where dreams take leap.
Rollercoaster climb, a breathless thrill,
Uncharted maps, potential's whispered fill.

Spotlights beckon, hearts a drumbeat's pace,
"What if's" alight, setting futures ablaze.
Adventure's seeds in fertile soil take root,
Winds of promise fill the sails, a daring loot.

Anticipation paints the world anew,
Each sunrise whispers: "What will we pursue?"
Stars like compass, hearts like compass true,
Excitement's melody, forever bright and new.

So let the butterflies dance, unafraid,
Embrace the whispers, dreams forever made.
For life's a canvas, waiting to be bold,
Where stories unfold, in futures yet untold.

~

## Contentment, Warmth, and Connection

They're the embers glowing in the hearth, casting a cozy glow against the winter's chill. Imagine the shared stories whispered under a starlit sky, the comforting weight of a loved one's hand in yours, the gentle rhythm of belonging that hums beneath the surface of our days. These are the quiet conversations woven from shared laughter and unspoken understanding, the refuge of souls intertwined, the anchor that holds us steady amidst life's turbulent waves.

*"Embers of Connection: A Hearthside Symphony"*

Hearthfire embers, glowing bright,
Chase winter's chill into the night.
Whispered stories, stars as eaves,
Shared laughter through the rustling leaves.

Hand in hand, a comforting weight,
Souls entwined, a trusting gate.
Gentle rhythms, whispers deep,
Belonging's song, where secrets sleep.

Quiet conversations, soft and light,
Weaving understanding, warm and bright.
Untethered words, a silent chime,
Reflecting depths in shared moonlit time.

Refuge found in woven trust,
An anchor holding, strong and just.
Through life's turbulent waves we flow,
Contentment's embers, soft and slow.

So open hearts to gentle light,
Let warmth embrace the fading night.
In connection's fire, forever burn,
A haven built, where spirits yearn.

## Compassion, Optimism, and Hope

They're the seeds of sunflowers, pushing through cracks in the pavement, yearning for the sun. Imagine the tears shed for another's pain, the unwavering belief in the possibility of something better, the tiny flicker of a candle refusing to be extinguished by the wind. These are the bridges we build across chasms of despair, the whispers of encouragement echoing through darkened alleyways, the gentle hands that lift when the burden becomes too heavy..

*"Petals of Compassion: Illuminating Shadows"*

Sunflowers sprout through cracks of grey.
Compassion's tears, a gentle spray.
For others' pain, a silent plea,
Hope's fragile flame, flickering free.

Candlelight against the storm,
Unwavering faith, forever warm.
Whispers of strength in darkened lanes,
Empowered hands that ease the pains.

Bridges built across despair's abyss,
Where optimism's melodies kiss.
Souls uplifted, burdens shared,
Compassion's touch, a burden spared.

In every act, a whispered song,
Hope's seeds take root, where they belong.
Empathy's hand, a guiding light,
Transforming darkness into bright.

Nurture hope's flame, let kindness bloom,
Building bridges, chasing shadows' gloom.
Will paint a world where tears refine,
And hearts united, forever shine.

## Sadness, Sorrow, and Grief

They're the raindrops whispering on windowpanes, blurring the edges of our world with a veil of grey. Imagine the empty chair at the table, a silent echo of laughter lost, the weight of tears streaming down unseen faces, the ache in our hearts that refuses to mend. These are the shadows that linger, reminding us of the fragility of life, the bittersweet beauty of impermanence, the depth of love etched in the lines of loss.

*"Whispers of Rain: Nurturing Grief into Growth"*

Rain whispers secrets on the pane,
Blurring edges, dimming flame.
An empty chair, a memory's hold,
Laughter's echo, bittersweet and cold.

Tears like rivers, silent streams,
Carving canyons in forgotten dreams.
Hearts that ache, refusing to mend,
Shadows linger, where stories end.

Fragile life, a whispered sigh,
Beauty veiled in tearful eye.
Impermanence, a poignant art,
Love's inscription in a breaking heart.

Yet in the hush, where sorrow weaves,
A tender strength the spirit keeps.
For memories bloom, like flowers in rain,
Love's legacy, that eases pain.

For in the depths of darkness sown,
Seeds of healing gently have grown.
Sadness whispers, then surrenders, free,
Leaving light where shadows used to be.

## Fear, Anxiety, and Apprehension

They're the shadows dancing on the wall, cast by an unseen flame. Imagine the trembling hands facing the unknown, the cold sweat of anticipation, the racing heart that mimics the drums of worry. These are the thorns that prick our skin, the whispers of doubt that gnaw at our confidence, the reminders of our vulnerability etched in the silence before the storm.

*"Courageous Whispers: Facing Shadows with Light"*

Shadows writhe on moonlit walls,
Cast by unseen, devouring falls.
Trembling hands, a silent plea,
Whispers of doubt, a gnawing sea.

Cold sweat beads, a fear-soaked crown,
Racing heart, a frantic drum, pounding down.
Thorns prick skin, a constant sting,
Anxiety's whispers, doubt they bring.

But in the hush, where shadows crawl,
Courage whispers, stands up tall.
Facing fears, with eyes set bright,
Embracing darkness, claiming light.

For even storms must lose their hold,
And sunlight paints a story bold.
Through trembling steps and whispered fears,
Resilience blooms, and silence clears.

So let the shadows dance their play,
Embrace the whispers, face the day.
With every breath, a victory won,
Fear's grip loosened; battle begun.

And when the sun breaks through the night,
You'll find yourself bathed in golden light.
For even in the dance of dark and dread,
Courage whispers, "Fear not," instead.

~

## Anger, Frustration, and Irritation

They're the storm clouds gathering on the horizon, pregnant with the threat of thunder. Imagine the clenched fists, the harsh words that sting like fire, the burning injustice that demands to be heard. These are the flames that threaten to consume, the echoes of hurt reverberating through shattered trust, the urgent need to reclaim power and set things right.

*"Embers of Empathy: Transforming Anger's Flames"*

Storm clouds gather, thick and low,
Anger's rumble, a pregnant flow.
Fists clench tight, a silent roar,
Harsh words sting, like flames that scorch and soar.

Flames lick high, threaten to consume,
Shattered trust, whispers in a darkened room.
But anger's fire, a double-edged blade,
Can heal or wound, a choice to be made.

For in the heat, where fury burns,
Compassion's embers, hope yearns.
Release the grip, let anger wane,
Forgive the hurt, ease the pain.

So let the storm clouds pass and fade,
Embrace the light, a gentler shade.
For in the dance of fire and rain,
Healing blossoms, once again.

Remember, anger's not a foe,
But a mirror, reflecting what we know.
With wisdom's hand, and open heart,
Transform the flames, a brand new start.

## Jealousy, Envy, and Covetousness

They're the weeds that snake through the garden, choking the vibrant blooms of contentment. Imagine the comparing eyes that diminish our own worth, the bitter taste of someone else's success, the longing for what we don't have. These are the vines that threaten to suffocate, the whispers of inadequacy that creep into our ears, the reminders that true happiness lies within, not in the shadows of another's light.

*"Blooms of Self-Discovery: Nurturing Gardens Within"*

Envy's shadow, long and thin,
Whispers doubts where blooms begin.
Comparing eyes, a thief of worth,
Stealing sunshine, dimming Earth.

Another's triumph, bitter wine,
Longing's vine, a twisted spine.
Covetousness, a grasping hand,
Choking contentment, barren land.

But hold, dear friend, and turn your gaze,
Within your garden, beauty ablaze.
Unfurl your petals, radiant hue,
Your own path blooms, just for you.

Let gratitude be fertile ground,
Where self-worth blossoms, strong and sound.
Comparison's weeds wither and fade,
Replaced by joy, a sunlit shade.

Celebrate the triumphs held,
Your victories, stories yet to be spelled.
Embrace the light, where you reside,
In your own garden, take pride.

So let envy's whispers softly drift,
Focus on roots, where blessings lift.
For happiness, a vibrant bloom,
Flourishes best in one's own room.

Remember, true joy finds its spark,
Not in shadows, but within your heart.
Cultivate the garden, tend the soul,
And watch your beauty make you whole.

~

## Apathy, Lack of Interest, and Lack of Motivation

They're the fog that descends, cloaking the world in a muted grey. Imagine the heavy limbs that refuse to move, the blank stare that reflects no spark of curiosity, the days that bleed into one another, devoid of colour or purpose. These are the silences that threaten to engulf us, the whispers of meaninglessness that drain our spirit, the reminders that even the sun casts a shadow if we stand still for too long.

*"Awakening from Apathy: Embracing the Symphony of Beginnings"*

A veil of fog descends, unseen,
Muffling laughter, dimming green.
Heavy limbs, like fallen trees,
No spark ignites, no spirit breathes.

Days bleed grey, a silent stream,
Purpose whispers, yet unheard, a dream.
Blank stares reflect the clouded sky,
Meaning's whispers lost in a sigh.

Even the sun casts a weary shade,
Where shadows linger, unafraid.
Apathy's grip, a chilling touch,
Silence echoes, "Not so much."

But wait, dear soul, a seed remains,
Hope's ember, whispering through the veins.
Reach within, where embers glow,
Let curiosity's gentle flame grow.

For in the stillness, voices rise,
A symphony of forgotten skies.
Listen close, to murmurs faint,
Apathy's fog begins to paint.

Step one foot, then another one,
Break the trance, the battle's won.
Small sparks ignite, a flickering pyre,
Motivation stirs, setting hearts on fire.

Chase the fog, with laughter's grace,
Embrace the sun, find warmth's embrace.
Rediscover colors, textures, sound,
In every breath, joy can be found.

So shake the silence, paint your day,
Apathy's whispers fade away.
For even in the dimmest light,
Your spark can conquer endless night.

Remember, stillness holds its own,
A chance to ponder, seeds to be sown.
But when the fog comes, don't succumb,
Rise and dance, let your spirit drum.

For apathy is not your end,
Apathy is where beginnings bend.
Embrace the pause, the quiet hour,
Then find your wings, rise with full power.

~

## Curiosity, Inquisitiveness, and Wonder

They're the wide eyes of a child, soaking in the world with insatiable thirst. Imagine the endless questions that probe the mysteries of life, the open heart that embraces the unknown, the joy of discovery that makes even the mundane an adventure. These are the keys that unlock hidden doors, the maps that guide us through uncharted territories, the reminders that the greatest treasures are often found not in seeking, but in the simple act of seeing.

*"Curiosity's Symphony: A Song of Endless Wonder"*

Wide eyes, mirrors to the sun,
Soak in stories, never done.
Endless questions pierce the veil,
Whispers yearning, seeking grail.

Open hearts, unfurled and bare,
Embrace the unknown, a whispered prayer.
Joy of discovery, a vibrant hum,
Makes mundane dance, keeps boredom numb.

Hidden doors creak, keys of wonder,
Unfurl maps unseen, chart paths asunder.
Through uncharted lands, curiosity strides,
Greatest treasures bloom where sight confides.

For not in seeking, grasping tight,
Do hearts find solace, bathe in light.
But in the seeing, open, free,
Beauty whispers, sets the spirit free.

Like fingertips on morning dew,
Curiosity paints worlds anew.
Wonder's brushstrokes, soft and bold,

Transform a pebble into purest gold.

So let your gaze be ever bright,
A child's delight, a starlit night.
Follow whispers, chase the spark,
Unravel mysteries, leave your mark.

For in the dance of what unfolds,
Curiosity whispers, "Never grow old."
Embrace the unknown, let wonder reign,
And find your magic in the simple grain.

Remember, eyes that never close,
See beyond the surface, where magic grows.
Keep your child's heart, forever young,
In curiosity's song, joy is sung.

~

## Calmness, Serenity, and Peace of Mind

They're the deep breaths that quiet the chatter of the mind, the gentle sway of trees in a quiet breeze, the stillness that allows us to simply be. Imagine the vast expanse of a starlit sky, the rhythm of the ocean washing ashore, the soft hum of a purring cat on a lap. These are the moments stolen from the frenetic dance of daily life, pockets of sanctuary where anxieties melt away like snowflakes in the sun. They are the pauses between notes in a melody, the spaces between brushstrokes on a canvas, the fertile ground where creativity and self-awareness blossom.

*"Harmony in Silence: Embracing Serenity's Whisper"*

Transform the flames, a brand new start.
Deep breaths hush the mind's loud drum,
A quiet breeze where stillness hums.
Like swaying trees in sunlit haze,
Serenity whispers, slows our pace.

Vast starlit sky, a canvas spread,
Where worries melt, anxieties shed.
Ocean's rhythm, soft and slow,
Washing worries' echo to and fro.

A purring cat, a gentle beat,
On sleepy laps, hearts find retreat.
Stolen moments, sanctuaries kept,
Where frenetic dance and burdens slept.

Pauses between notes, a silent space,
Brushstrokes resting, finding grace.
Fertile ground, where visions bloom,
Creativity whispers, chasing gloom.

In calmness' hold, self-awareness gleams,
A diamond found in moonlit streams.

Serene reflections, clear and bright,
Shine inner wisdom, bathed in light.

So let the world's loud chorus fade,
Embrace the hush, no longer afraid.
For in these pockets, pure and true,
The soul finds solace, born anew.

Breathe deep, dear friend, and let it be,
The dance of stillness, setting you free.
In quietude, where peace resides,
Your life's own melody confides.

Remember, moments of calm untold,
Are threads of gold, more precious than gold.
Hold these treasures close within,
And watch your spirit softly spin.

For calmness is not just a pause,
But a refuge built with unseen laws.
A sanctuary, where you can soar,
Forevermore, forevermore.

~

## Acceptance, Understanding, and Embracing Reality

They're the whispers of wisdom etched in the lines of a weathered face, the gentle acceptance of the sun setting after a glorious day, the courage to look at life through unclouded eyes. Imagine the gentle surrender to what is, the release of resistance that drains our strength, the quiet knowing that some things are simply beyond our control. These are the bridges we build between expectations and reality, the open arms that hold both light and shadow, the reminders that true resilience lies not in fighting the tide, but in learning to flow with it.

*"Whispers of Wisdom: Embracing the Dance of Light and Shadow"*

Transform the flames, a brand new start.
Wisdom whispers in weathered lines,
Sun's descent, acceptance entwines.
Open eyes, unflinching sight,
Embrace reality, hold it tight.

Gentle surrender, a whispered plea,
Release resistance, set your spirit free.
Knowing's quiet, a whispered chime,
Some things flow, beyond control's tight rhyme.

Between expectation's painted dream,
And reality's unfiltered stream,
We build bridges, strong and true,
Holding light and shadow, me and you.

Open arms, embracing all,
Sunshine's warmth and winter's squall.
For true resilience isn't might,
But flowing with the tide, taking flight.

So let the waves crest, then gently fall,
Yielding to nature's mighty call.

In acceptance's cradle, find your way,
Where shadows dance, and sunbeams play.

Understand the ebb and flow,
The tapestry of life, where stories grow.
Embrace the imperfections, flaws and all,
For beauty blooms in answer to your call.

Remember, strength in yielding lies,
Letting go of battles in disguise.
Flow with the current, wise, and bold,
And find your peace, in stories untold.

Like ancient rivers, winding free,
Acceptance whispers, "Just be, just be."
In harmony with life's untamed grace,
Discover hidden strength, find your rightful place.

For the world unfolds in vibrant hues,
When we embrace reality and choose.
To dance with shadows, bathe in light,
And claim the power of accepting night.

~

# Sentiments

Whispering beneath the surface are our sentiments, the hidden biases and inclinations that shape our perspectives. This discussion delves into the power of these subtle slants, exploring how they influence our judgments and interpretations of the world around us. Understanding our own sentiments is crucial for fostering empathy and building bridges with others.

While emotions are the raw notes, feelings are the interpretive melodies, and sentiments are the final judgment, all three are intertwined in the grand opera of human experience. Each term plays a crucial role in shaping our interactions with the world, and understanding their subtle differences can enrich our understanding of ourselves and others. In the dance of human experience, emotions, feelings, and sentiments pirouette in a delicate ballet, often blurring their steps and leaving us wondering about the differences. While all three play a vital role in our inner lives, they each hold distinct positions on the stage.

Emotions are the fiery dancers, the primal forces that erupt from our depths. Rooted in biology, they trigger physiological changes like racing hearts and flushed cheeks, painting our faces with the colors of joy, sadness, anger, or fear. These universal melodies, shared across cultures, are the core notes of our human symphony.

Feelings, on the other hand, are the introspective observers, the mindful companions who whisper interpretations of the emotional symphony. They are the conscious reflections of our internal storms, weaving narratives around the raw sensations of emotions. While the joy of a delicious cake might be the emotional melody, the feeling might be a warm contentment that lingers like a sweet aftertaste.

Finally, sentiments are the seasoned critics, the evaluative judges who assess the overall performance. They are informed by our personal experiences, beliefs, and values, guiding us to form positive or negative judgments about the world around us. The delicious cake might not only evoke feelings of joy and contentment, but also a positive sentiment towards the baker or the occasion it celebrates.

So, while emotions light the fire, feelings interpret the flames, and sentiments offer the final verdict, all three are essential components of our emotional landscape. They work together to shape our experiences, guide our decisions, and connect us to the world around us.

## Sentiments: Revealing the Depths of Perception

Beneath the surface of conscious thought lies a labyrinth of sentiments, those intricate whispers that shape individual perspectives. This exploration delves into the profound influence of these subtle inclinations, unravelling the threads that colour judgments and interpretations. Understanding these nuances becomes a guiding compass, fostering empathy and connection across the diverse landscapes of human experience.

*"Whispers of the Heart: Navigating the Labyrinth of Sentiments"*

Where conscious thought in sunlit streams doth flow,
Beneath it ripples a hidden undertow.
A labyrinth of whispers, soft and deep,
Where sentiments in shadowed chambers sleep.

These subtle tendrils, with each beat of heart,
Unfold the tapestry, where we play our part.
Judgments arise, like brushstrokes on a wall,
Coloured by whispers, destined to enthral.

Emotions thunder, lightning in the eye,
A primal dance, where joys and sorrows lie.
Feelings follow, echoes in the soul,
Conscious echoes, making stories whole.

Sentiments then, the wise and watchful guide,
From hidden biases, they gently glide.
Distilling essence, weaving threads unseen,
Shaping landscapes, where minds and hearts convene.

Empathy blossoms, nurtured by this light,
A bridge of understanding, bathed in moonlit night.
Across the vast expanse of humankind,
These whispered echoes help us truly find.

The common ground, the shared and precious hue,
Where differences dance, in shades of me and you.
So let us listen to the symphony within,
Where sentiments unravel, the story starts to spin.

For in this knowledge, woven like a shroud,
We find the compass, leading ever proud,
Through tangled paths, where darkness seeks to hide,
Toward the solace of connection, deep inside.

~

## Uncovering Unseen Currents: Whispers of Bias

Exploring the covert currents under the surface, one unveils the realm of biases, silent architects of individual perceptions. By shining a light on these hidden inclinations, individuals confront and transform biases into opportunities for personal growth. Acknowledging and comprehending biases becomes a tool for promoting inclusivity and understanding in the grand tapestry of human interactions.

*"Unmasking Currents: Navigating the Waters of Hidden Biases"*

Beneath the calm waters of conscious thought,
Unseen currents whisper, biases wrought.
Like hidden reefs, they shape the ocean's flow,
Bending perceptions, where judgements grow.

These silent architects, with unseen hand,
Craft frames of colour, for what we understand.
The lens of bias, tinted ever bright,
Casts skewed reflections on the world's vast light.

But courage whispers, a beacon in the tide,
To dive beneath the surface, where shadows hide.
To grapple with the depths, where biases lie,
And bring them forth, to meet the questioning eye.

For in acknowledging these hidden streams,
We claim the power to rewrite our dreams.
To break the chains of prejudice and fear,
And build a bridge of understanding, clear.

No longer victims of the currents' sway,
We become architects, shaping a brighter day.
With empathy as compass, and truth as guide,
We chart a course where biases subside.

So let the whispers rise, unmasked and bold,
No longer secrets, stories to be told.
For in vulnerability, connection thrives,
And inclusivity blooms, where understanding strives.

Together then, we weave a richer hue,
Where differences dance, and biases anew,
Transformed from shadows, to stepping stones,
Toward a world where every heart truly owns,

The freedom to see, with eyes unclouded, vast,
The beauty of oneness, holding shadows fast.
Uncovering currents, whispering no more,
We build a world where biases empower, not distort.

~

## The Artistry of Subconscious Slants: Moulding Perspectives

Embark on a journey through the artistry of subconscious inclinations, where the shaping of perspectives takes place. This exploration unravels the interplay between the subconscious and the external world, illustrating how subtle biases influence the lenses through which individuals perceive reality. Recognizing these influences opens avenues for refining perspectives, fostering a more empathetic understanding of the multifaceted human experience.

*"Canvas of Shadows: Unveiling the Artistry of Biases"*

In realms unseen, where shadows softly sway,
A hidden studio bathes in moonlit grace,
There, biases like sculptors hold their sway,
Moulding perspectives, leaving their embrace.

Subconscious whispers, threads of memory spun,
Weave subtle filters, tinting what we see,
Childhood echoes, fears beneath the sun,
Societal hues, shaping silently.

Through tinted lenses, landscapes shift and bend,
Familiar vistas taking twisted forms,
Judgments arise, where stories misinterpret,
In shades of bias, weathering through storms.

But dawn ignites, a gentle, searching light,
That casts its glow within the hidden hall,
We glimpse the artist, bathed in inner sight,
Shaping the canvas, master of it all.

No longer puppets to the whispers' snare,
We grasp the brush, reclaim the power held,
To shift the filters, paint a canvas fair,
Where empathy's light the shadows can dispel.

With borrowed lenses, let compassion guide,
Across the chasms built by misunderstanding,
In shared perspectives, common ground we find,
A symphony of stories, hearts expanding.

So let the artist, freed from shadows' hold,
Embrace the spectrum, with a bolder hue,
Each slant and filter, a story to be told,
A tapestry where differences shine through.

With hearts unveiled, and lenses newly clear,
We paint a world where understanding thrives,
Where biases, transformed, no longer leer,
But guide the dance where every spirit strives.

In this embrace, where light and shadow blend,
We find the masterpiece, a radiant hue,
Where every slant, with every fiber fine,
Whispers a truth, forever born anew.

~

# Expressions

Words, though profound, are not the sole ink residing in a poet's well. The subtleties of your head's tilt, the dance of your smile's twitch, the blaze within your gaze; these are brushstrokes that articulate when words stumble. It beckons you to master the language of your body, the rhythm of your sighs, and the ballet of your hands. Each movement crafts a stanza in the silent poem of your existence, harbouring concealed meanings waiting to unfold.

Expressions, far from being isolated notes, weave a intricate tapestry where each element intertwines, unveiling the richness and depth of our inner world. To fathom the delicate connections between expressions, emotions, feelings, and sentiments is to gain a profound insight into the human experience. It grants us the capacity to forge connections with others that transcend the superficial.

At the core of every being resonates a symphony—a vibrant composition echoing a kaleidoscope of emotions, feelings, and sentiments. The challenge lies in expressing this intricate melody to the world. Here enters the eloquent tapestry of expressions—facial nuances, corporeal whispers, and spoken melodies converge to become the language of our soul. These expressions transcend the confines of words, creating a bridge between the inner symphony and the external world, inviting others to partake in the beauty and complexity of our shared human experience.

*"Expressions Unveiled: A Tapestry of Human Souls"*

In realms unseen, where thoughts take flight,
A silent symphony hums, bathed in light.
Emotions dance, a vibrant choir,

Feelings echo, setting hearts afire.

Expressions bloom, a tapestry wide,
Where brushstrokes whisper what words can't hide.
Faces like canvases, emotions bright,
Furrowed brows, smiles taking flight.

Eyes, windows to the soul within,
Reflecting storms, where joy can spin.
Body language, a silent script,
Leaning in, a bond to grip.

Spoken words, a melody's thread,
Whispering secrets, gently said.
Inflections rise, like notes on air,
Painting landscapes, painted with care.

Empathy's brush, a gentle touch,
Connects the threads, means so much.
In shared expressions, stories unfold,
Understanding whispers, warm and bold.

From fleeting glances to laughter's chime,
Each gesture speaks, beyond space and time.
A tapestry woven, rich and deep,
Where human hearts in unison leap.

So, listen close, to the silent hum,
The language of souls, where all become.
In expressions' echo, softly sung,
A symphony of hearts, forever young.

For in the dance of light and shade,
Where secrets bloom, unafraid,
We find the beauty, shared and true,
The tapestry of me, woven with you.

~

## Facial Expressions

Facial expressions are the universal canvases upon which our emotions paint their first strokes. A raised eyebrow, a furrowed brow, a mischievous grin; these are instant snapshots of our inner landscapes, understood across cultures and languages. They act as emotional echoes, mirroring the storms brewing within, whether a flush of shame's blush or the softening eyes of contentment. But this isn't a one-way street; facial expressions can also influence our feelings. A forced smile, for instance, can trick our brain into releasing feel-good chemicals, gradually shifting our internal weather.

*"Skin Symphony: Unveiling Emotions on the Canvas of Faces"*

Upon the canvas, where skin meets air,
Emotions dance, a fleeting fair.
No brushstrokes needed, no palette grand,
Just muscles twitching, by nature's hand.

A raised eyebrow, a question's sting,
A furrowed brow, where worries cling.
A mischievous grin, a playful spark,
Eyes that soften, leaving darkness stark.

These fleeting strokes, a silent tongue,
Across cultures, feelings are sung.
No need for words, the story's plain,
In joy's bright smile, or sorrow's rain.

Shame's blush blooms, a crimson stain,
Contentment's sigh, a gentle refrain.
Mirrors of the soul, emotions flare,
Reflected landscapes, painted there.

But not just echoes, these brushstrokes bold,

Can shape the feelings, young and old.
A forced smile's curve, a trick of light,
Can coax the sun, through clouds of night.

So watch the dance, on skin so thin,
The whispers painted, where hearts begin.
In every twitch, a story told,
The tapestry of faces, young and old.

For in these lines, where laughter plays,
And shadows linger, through passing days,
We find the truth, laid bare and bright,
The silent symphony, in shades of light.

~

## Universal Language

Our faces serve as billboards, displaying a universal language of emotions understood across cultures. A raised eyebrow might signal curiosity, a furrowed brow concern, and a wide smile joy. These innate expressions provide instant glimpses into our emotional states.

*"Faces of the Silent Symphony: A Universal Language"*

Beyond the painted city's din,
A silent whisper starts to spin.
Eyes, wide mirrors, reflect the soul,
Where joy ignites, and shadows stroll.

A raised brow arches, curiosity's sting,
A furrowed crease, where worries cling.
A smile, a crescent, joy unbound,
Laughter's melody, on faces found.

Tears, like diamonds, softly trace,
The weight of sorrow, etched with grace.
Though tongues may differ, words may stray,
These silent brushstrokes light the way.

This language spoken, not in sound,
Across all lands, on common ground.
No borders hold, no barriers rise,
In shared emotions, humanity wise.

For beyond spoken word, masks, and guise,
In every glance, a truth sunrise.
The unspoken stories, etched so deep,
The universal language, we all keep.

~

## Emotional Echoes

Facial expressions serve as the eloquent ambassadors of our innermost emotions, bearing witness to the intricate symphony playing within the chambers of our soul. When embarrassment knocks at the door, our cheeks become the canvas painted with the blush of vulnerability, a vivid proclamation of our emotional state. In the face of anger, our jaws tighten like a fortress, holding back the tempest within.

On the contrary, when contentment graces our being, our features soften into a serene landscape, revealing the calm after the storm. These expressions are not mere surface reflections but rather real-time revelations, offering a candid glimpse into the emotional weather patterns shaping the landscape of our internal world. Each subtle shift, a brushstroke on the canvas of our face, narrates the ongoing story of our inner turmoil and tranquillity.

*"Heart's Symphony: The Unspoken Language of Emotions"*

Beneath the skin, where shadows play,
A symphony of hearts takes sway.
Emotions ripple, waves unseen,
Echoing outward, on faces keen.

A blush unfurls, a crimson tide,
Where shame ignites, and secrets hide.
Jaws clench tight, a storm descends,
As anger's fist within ascends.

Eyes soften, shadows gently fall,
Contentment's embrace, a welcome thrall.
A smile unfurls, a sunlit bloom,
Joy's echo dancing, dispelling gloom.

These whispered signals, swift and pure,
Unveil the storms that hearts endure.

Each wrinkle etched, a whispered line,
Emotional echoes, making hearts entwined.

Do watch the dance, on skin so thin,
Where hidden melodies always begin.
In every twitch says, a story untold,
The silent symphony, of hearts laid bold.

~

## Feelings Reflected

Facial expressions, far from being passive mirrors of our emotions, possess the remarkable ability to wield influence over the very feelings they reflect. A forced smile, orchestrated consciously, becomes a silent conductor orchestrating a symphony of biochemical reactions within the confines of our brain. As the corners of our lips curve upward, the brain responds by releasing a cascade of feel-good chemicals, a clandestine alchemy that gradually transforms our internal state. In this intricate dance between expression and emotion, a simple smile becomes a catalyst, coaxing the emergence of joy and warmth from the depths of our being.

*"Mirrors of Emotion: The Dance Behind Faces"*

Behind the eyes, where shadows weave,
A silent dance, emotions breathe.
But smiles are mirrors, not just glass,
They bend the light, and let feelings pass.

Laughter's echo, so bright and free,
Can chase away any unpervert misery.
A furrowed brow, with purpose set,
Can forge the strength, no tears have met.

These fleeting masks, we wear each day,
Not just reflections, but the way.
They sculpt the narratives as we hold,
moulding stories, too brave and bold.

Now lift your chin, and let eyes shine,
Though darkness lingers, intertwined.
For faces sing, a silent inner song,
And shape the world, where we belong.

~

## Body Language

Body language becomes an intricate dance of unspoken communication, often revealing truths that words attempt to cloak. A slouched posture whispers of a burden carried, a narrative of subdued emotions etched in the curve of the spine. The folding of arms constructs a barricade, an unspoken shield against intrusion into the inner sanctum of thoughts.

Conversely, an open stance paints a portrait of confidence, a canvas where assurance and self-possession brushstroke the air. These subtle cues act as leaks of emotion, unravelling what our spoken language might endeavour to conceal. Fidgeting hands lay bare the tremors of nervousness, averted eyes sketch discomfort, and a clenched fist subtly echoes the quiet rage within.

Leaning in during conversation orchestrates an overture of interest, while maintaining distance orchestrates a silent sonnet of indifference. And in the realm of connectivity, mirroring someone's posture becomes a bridge of resonance, an unspoken accord composed in the shared language of unspoken gestures.

*"Symphony of Unveiling Through Postures"*

From slouched spines to outstretched hand,
A silent chorus, across the land.
Emotions ripple, not in sound,
But postures echo, all around.

A clenched fist, a storm suppressed,
Anger simmers, in unrest.
Crossing fingers, silent prayer,
Hope's embers glow, in anxious air.

These fleeting brushstrokes, on human clay,
Reveal the landscapes, where true feelings play.
A whispered dialogue, without a word,
Body language, the soul, unstirred.

listen in close, to the silent beat,
The rhythm of hearts, in motion meet.
In postures painted, soft and bold,
We find the beauty, of stories untold.

~

## Unspoken Dialogue

Body language is a nuanced symphony of silent expressions that transcends verbal communication, enriching the narrative of our emotions. The subtle artistry of our posture, gestures, and even the cadence of our steps paints an intricate mural of unspoken sentiments. A slouched posture becomes the brushstroke of a melancholy canvas, a visual poetry conveying the weight of sorrows.

Crossed arms craft a defensive fortress, an unyielding structure shielding vulnerabilities. In contrast, an open stance unfolds as the anthem of confidence, an expansive portrayal of self-assurance. This non-verbal layer of communication serves as a harmonious companion to spoken words, either accentuating their resonance or weaving a counterpoint that challenges their meaning.

Every movement becomes a note, contributing to the symphony of our unspoken language, resonating with the melody of our deepest emotions.

*"Wordless Dialogues: The Art of Body Language"*

No need for words, no scripted phrase,
The body speaks, in countless ways.
A slouch that whispers unspoken woes,
Crossed arms that build defensive walls, they pose.

Open stance invites the world to stay,
Confident strides march into the fray.
Leaning in, a whispered vow,
Secrets shared, in hearts somehow.

Fidgeting hands betray the inner storm,
Averted eyes where shadows swarm.
Clenched fists hold anger tightly bound,
Unleashed emotions, on silent ground.

Fingertips tap, a restless beat,
Anticipation's whispers, bittersweet.
Mirrored smiles, a joyful chime,
Harmony found, in the perfect time.

Do watch the dance, the silent play,
Unravel stories, day by day.
In every shift, a truth laid bare,
The unspoken dialogue, hanging in the air.

~

## Emotional Leakage

While we can try to mask our emotions with our words, our body language often betrays our true feelings. Despite our efforts to cloak emotions with carefully chosen words, the subtle nuances of our physical expressions betray the authentic narratives within. The restless choreography of fidgeting hands becomes a telltale sign, unravelling the threads of nervousness woven beneath the surface. Averted eyes, like a compass diverting attention, cast light upon the discomfort concealed beneath spoken phrases.

Similarly, a clenched fist becomes a visual crescendo, resonating with suppressed anger as a silent reverberation of the emotional tempest beneath. These nuanced cues function as windows, granting others a glimpse into the rich tapestry of emotions simmering beneath the facade, transforming unspoken gestures into profound revelations.

*"Whispers Within: Emotions Unveiled"*

From trembling lips to furrowed brow,
Emotions spill, somehow, somehow.
No dam can hold, no wall withstands,
The tidal surge, of heart and hand.

A sigh escapes, a weary moan,
Burden carried, all alone.
Feet that shuffle, lost and slow,
Despair's echoes, softly flow.

Laughter rings, a joyous chime,
Sunlight dancing, in perfect time.
Heads held high, with purpose set,
Confidence marches, without regret.

These whispered tremors, on skin so thin,

Speak volumes louder, than words within.
Emotional leakage, raw and bright,
Painting landscapes, bathed in inner light.

So listen close, to the silent hum,
The rhythm of souls, overcoming.
In leakage echoes, soft and bold,
We find the beauty, in stories untold.

~

## Sentiment Compass

Body language extends beyond the realm of fleeting emotions, providing a nuanced portrayal of our overarching sentiments and attitudes. Leaning in during a conversation becomes a visual ode to interest, a subtle gesture that echoes the engagement of one's thoughts.

On the other hand, maintaining a calculated distance speaks volumes about a sentiment of indifference, creating an unspoken barrier that shields one's emotional space. Mirroring someone's posture emerges as a silent dance of camaraderie, an unconscious effort to bridge the gap and foster a positive rapport.

*"Silent Choreography: The Language of Body Whispers"*

Beyond the flicker of a fleeting mood,
Body whispers tales, misunderstood.
Not just emotions, shadows swift,
But judgments etched, in posture's shift.

Leaning in, a bridge takes flight,
Interest whispers, bathed in light.
Distance lingers, cold and stark,
Indifference etched, beneath the bark.

Mirrored movements, hearts entwined,
Rapports' reflection softly signed.
Crossed arms a wall, suspicion's shield,
Disapproval's echo, unrevealed.

watching this dance, of the silent tide,
Where sentiments flow, side by side.
In every sway, a story is told,
The compass hidden, brave and bold.

## The Spoken Word

In the vibrant tapestry of human expression, the spoken word emerges as a melody unlike any other. It isn't just a sequence of syllables or a tool for conveying information; it's the vocal chords of our inner symphony, weaving emotions into vibrant sonic landscapes. Through it, joy bursts forth in infectious laughter, sorrow spills in heartbroken whispers, and anger crackles like lightning in a storm.

But the spoken word isn't merely a reflection of our internal states; it's a sculptor of them as well. Words brush strokes of gratitude onto the canvas of our hearts, cultivating contentment where doubts once festered. Conversely, the dark whispers of self-criticism can etch lines of negativity, casting long shadows onto our self-image. In a potent alchemy, the very act of speaking becomes a shaping force, moulding the contours of our inner worlds and influencing the realities we experience.

Imagine entering a bustling marketplace, a cacophony of voices swirling around you. A street vendor's call rings out, a passionate aria brimming with the promise of juicy mangoes. Across the way, a hushed conversation between lovers unfolds, their words like velvet cloaks draped around intimate sentiments. A child's excited chatter, tinged with awe, narrates the wonders of a nearby puppet show. Each voice, unique in its texture and tone, paints a distinct emotional portrait, weaving a rich tapestry of human experience.

This kaleidoscope of sound underscores the immense power of language. A single phrase, meticulously chosen, can ignite a revolution or soothe a grieving soul. A well-timed joke can break the tension in a room, while a heartfelt apology can mend a fractured relationship. Words weave bridges between hearts, allowing us to share the intricate landscapes of our inner worlds and find connection in the shared language of emotion.

Yet, this power demands responsibility. Just as words can build, they can also break. Unkind pronouncements can leave scars that linger long after the echo fades. Careless gossip can spread like wildfire, leaving a trail of devastation in its wake. We must wield this potent tool with mindfulness, choosing our words with the same reverence as a musician selects each note in their composition.

Ultimately, the spoken word is a gift, a potent instrument entrusted to each of us. By harnessing its power with awareness and empathy, we can create a symphony of understanding, connection, and positive change. Let us speak not just to be heard, but to listen, to connect, and to sculpt a world where words become bridges of healing, understanding, and shared humanity.

*"The Spoken Symphony of Emotion"*

From hushed confessions, secrets kept,
To soaring speeches, where dreams take flight,
The spoken word, a boundless tide,
Washing over, where feelings hide.

Love's sonnet, a whispered vow,
Tender promises, on moonlit bough.
Passion's tango, a burning fire,
Rhythm of hearts, in fierce desire.

Doubt's discordant tune, a jarring chime,
Dissonance echoes, eroding time.
Hope's triumphant hymn, a clarion call,
Rallying spirits, through winter's thrall.

So guard your tongue, a sacred lyre,
Let language dance, with kindled fire.
For spoken music, whispers truth,
A symphony of hearts, in eternal youth.

~

## Articulating the Intangible

Words give voice to the invisible world within. Through carefully chosen phrases and the tone of our voice, we can express joy, sorrow, anger, or any other emotion in a nuanced and specific way. Language allows us to paint detailed pictures of our inner landscapes.

*"Words Unbound: A Symphony of Expression"*

From trembling lips to laughter's chime,
Words dance and sing, across space and time.
No chisel cold, no sculptor's hand,
Just stories spun, on common sand.

Hope's fragile dawn, with sunrise hue,
In tender phrases, born anew.
Despair's abyss, a starless night,
Woven in darkness, whispered tight.

With every turn, a twist, a bend,
The inner journey, words transcend.
From whispered secrets, close and deep,
To public roars, where dreams take leap.

This vibrant tapestry, words entwine,
A shared language, truly divine.
Articulating soul of what's within,
The human symphony, dance, and spin.

~

## Shaping Feelings and Sentiments

The human voice, an instrument of astonishing versatility, not only echoes the emotions within, but also possesses the power to sculpt and mould them. Our words, like notes on a musical scale, can evoke a kaleidoscope of feelings, from joy's effervescent laughter to sorrow's tear-stained whispers. But the resonance of language goes beyond mere reflection; it becomes an active force, shaping the very landscape of our inner world.

Imagine a heart brimming with gratitude, like a fertile field bathed in golden sunlight. As we express this gratitude in heartfelt words, we nourish its seeds, making contentment bloom in our souls. Conversely, the seeds of negativity sown by self-criticism can take root in the fertile soil of our minds, casting long shadows of doubt and insecurity. Words become the gardener's tools, tilling the soil of our emotions and tending to the delicate seedlings of our inner world.

The power of language extends beyond individual feelings, weaving the fabric of our overall sentiments. A whispered encouragement can bridge the chasm of despair, igniting a spark of hope in another's heart. Conversely, a carelessly flung barb can fester into a wound of resentment, altering the very course of a relationship. Words become the threads on the loom of our lives, weaving tapestries of joy and sorrow, connection and isolation, woven into the intricate fabric of human experience.

*"Melodies of the Voice: Weaving Words with Wisdom"*

The human voice, a violin of soul,
Strums chords of feeling, takes on whole
The range of passions, whispering fears,
Or roaring triumphs, drying years.

Words, seeds they are, on fertile ground,
Of gratitude, where joy resounds.
But thorns of doubt, in shadows sown,
By self-critique, alone, unknown.

A bridge of hope, a whispered phrase,
Can lift a heart from sorrow's haze.
While careless tongues, like wildfires spread,
Leave ashes where connection bled.

This loom of language, threads of fate,
We weave our tapestries, intricate.
With mindful hands, and tender care,
Let love's soft hues be woven there.

For words, they hold a double blade,
To heal or wound, serenade.
So, choose with wisdom, wield with grace,
And paint a world where beauties embraced.

~

## Building Bridges and Walls

The way we speak can foster connection or create distance. Empathetic and understanding language builds bridges, while harsh or dismissive words erect walls. Our choice of words reflects not just our emotions but also our values and our desire to connect with others.

*"Threads of Connection: Weaving Conversations with Care"*

From furrowed brows to eyes that shine,
A conversation's tapestry, entwine.
Kindness spoken, a gentle thread,
Hope's fragile tendrils, softly spread.

Respect's embrace, a sturdy beam,
On which understanding's trust can stream.
Humours' brushstrokes, light and bright,
Fill the canvas, banishing night.

But cutting words, like blades they fall,
Severing threads and building a wall.
Anger's embers, spitting flame,
Consume connection, whispers of blame.

In every syllable, a choice we make,
To build a haven, or hearts to break.
Let bridges bloom, with careful art,
And mend the walls, with a mindful heart.

~

## The Brushstrokes of the Soul: Through Body and Face

From the internal to the external, focusing on how we express our inner symphony through body and face. It delves into the language of nonverbal communication, deciphering the meaning behind dancing eyebrows, a quivering voice, or a shy smile.

*"Whispers Unveiled: The Language of Silent Symphony"*

Beyond the spoken word, a symphony resides,
Emotions dancing, where no voice confides.
But from the depths, a brush begins to trace,
On canvas vast, the soul's unspoken grace.

The body whispers, in a silent tongue,
A language woven, where secrets are sprung.
From furrowed brows, where worry casts its shade,
To eyes alight, with dreams unfurled and played.

The hands they tremble, with unspoken fear,
While fingers tap, anticipation near.
A clenched fist speaks, of anger held too tight,
And open palms embrace the coming light.

The feet they shuffle, lost in doubt's despair,
While dancing steps proclaim a joy to share.
A tilted head, curiosity's embrace,
And closed eyes hide, a smile upon the face.

The face, a map where shadows interweave,
A landscape etched, where joys and sorrows grieve.
A quivering lip, confessions yet untold,
A furrowed brow, where wisdom's flag unfolds.

A dancing eyebrow, playful and unmasked,
A furrowed line, where trust has been unasked.
A shy smile blooming, like a rose in spring,

And tearful eyes, where unspoken stories cling.

The blush that paints a canvas flushed with shame,
A laugh that ripples, like a whispered flame.
Each brushstroke sings, a silent melody,
The soul's true language, for all the world to see.

Do learn to listen, to this unspoken tongue,
The whispers etched, where secrets lie unsung.
For in the dance of body, face, and hand,
We find the echoes, of a heart's command.

~

## The Eyes Speak Volumes: Decoding Emotional Cues

In the vast canvas of the human face, the eyes hold center stage, luminous pools reflecting the soul's intricate play. More than mere organs of sight, they become windows, whispering secrets and painting emotions with a single glance. To learn the language of the eyes is to unlock a hidden world, where unspoken stories dance in the depths.

Imagine, for a moment, a gaze that lingers, warm and steady. It speaks of trust, of connection forged in silent understanding. A fleeting glance, darting and nervous, whispers anxieties, secrets yet to be confessed. Eyes wide with wonder, like a child's at a starlit sky, reveal an open heart, embracing life's magic.

The dance of the pupils, too, tells a tale. Dilated in the glow of interest, they beckon you closer, inviting deeper exploration. Constricted in the grip of fear, they shrink inward, seeking refuge from the world's harshness. Downcast and heavy, they bear the weight of sadness, a silent plea for solace.

To truly decode the language of the eyes, we must become attentive observers, not just of their movements and expressions, but of the context in which they unfold. A furrowed brow in isolation may signify anger, but paired with a tilted head, it could be curiosity. A fleeting glance away may be shyness, or perhaps a moment of introspection.

Learning to read the eyes is a journey of empathy, a constant dance of observation and understanding. It requires us to step beyond our own assumptions and tune into the subtle nuances that whisper beneath the surface.

*"Eyes Unveiled: The Silent Language of Emotion"*

Where secrets bloom, unafraid,
In the depths of eyes, untold stories dwell,
Mirrors reflecting, what words conceal.
No brushstrokes needed, no whispered tongue,
Emotions flicker, where secrets are sprung.

A gaze unwavering, locked in deep embrace,
Speaks of trust and love, etched on the face.
Eyes wide with wonder, curiosity's call,
Thirsting for knowledge, embracing all.

A soft, averted glance, a shy delight,
Holds whispers of longing, bathed in gentle light.
Eyes narrowed, sharp, a flicker of disdain,
A silent judgement, whispered like the rain.

Tears that well and spill, like rivers overflowing,
Tell tales of sorrow, where hearts are grieving.
Laughter sparkling, a sunlit summer stream,
Washes away troubles, in a joyous dream.

Pupils dilated, fear's cold hand takes hold,
Wide and watchful, in stories yet untold.
Eyes downcast, shame's cloak hangs heavy and low,
Hiding confessions, where secrets softly flow.

But learn to read, beyond the surface gleam,
For subtle tremors, whisper what they seem.
A fleeting flicker, a hidden spark,
The language of eyes, leaves its subtle mark.

~

## Unveiling the Dance of Expression: From Smiles to Tears

Life unfolds in a kaleidoscope of faces, a silent symphony where emotions pirouette across skin and bone. From the fleeting sunbeam of a laugh to the pearl-drop sorrow of a tear, our expressions are a mesmerizing performance, revealing the hidden world within.

A smile, a brushstroke of joy, paints the canvas of our face. It curves lips like crescents, crinkles eyes with mischievous delight, and sends ripples of warmth outward, melting barriers and forging connections. In that simple arc, we offer a piece of our sunlit soul, inviting others to bask in its glow.

Laughter, a cascading melody, erupts from the depths of joy. It bubbles through lips, tinkles in eyes, and shakes the very frame of our being. It's a contagious storm, sweeping away shadows and uniting hearts in a shared symphony of light. In laughter, we find a universal language, a bridge built on pure delight.

But the dance of expression isn't confined to joy. Sorrow, a whispered sigh, leaves its mark in eyes misted with rain. Tears, like liquid diamonds, spill from the well of the soul, tracing silent stories on our cheeks. In these glistening drops, we find a raw vulnerability, a glimpse into the tender depths of our humanity.

Anger, a storm cloud gathering, tightens fists and furrows brows. It flashes in narrowed eyes and trembles in a clenched jaw. It's a potent force, demanding attention, urging action. In the fiery language of anger, we find the need for boundaries, the strength to defend our truth.

Fear, a whisper in the dark, paints the face with a pallor of uncertainty. Widened eyes search for solace, while trembling hands betray the unease within. In this silent terror, we find the raw instinct for survival, the primal urge to flee or fight.

But our expressions are not mere masks, passive reflections of our inner turmoil. They are active participants, shaping our experiences and influencing those around us. A confident smile can disarm doubt, a teardrop can elicit empathy, and a laugh can break down walls. In the dance of expression, we find not just revelation, but transformation.

*"The Silent Ballet of Emotion"*

A stage unfurls, not wood nor brick,
But canvas vast, of flesh so quick.
From sunrise gleam of laughter's chime,
To moonlit tear, that whispers time.

A smile, a brushstroke light and bright,
Paints joy's embrace, on morning's light.
Eyes dancing stars, on cheeks that bloom,
A silent symphony, within the room.

A furrowed brow, a shadow cast,
Where worry lingers, secrets fast.
Lips pursed tight, a silent plea,
For understanding, empathy.

A raised eyebrow, mischief's call,
A playful whisper, breaching all.
Nose crinkled up, in joyful scorn,
At silly jests, and laughter born.

A quivering chin, a tear's descent,
Where sorrows gather, hearts bereft.
Eyes welling pools, reflecting pain,
A silent language, spoken plain.

But in this dance, not steps alone,
A rhythm woven, skin and bone.
The tilt of head, a trust confessed,
Crossed arms, a wall against the rest.

Each fleeting twitch, a whispered tale,
Emotions etched, without a veil.
For in this ballet, raw and true,
Our inner landscapes come to view.

As we watch the waltz, sway and spin,
The stories get etched, beneath our skin.
From smiles that bridge, to tears that mend,
This tapestry of expression, without end.

~

## The Power of Storytelling

Stories are the lifeblood of this canvas, the threads that weave our emotions, feelings, and senses into a cohesive narrative. Weave tapestries of words, paint landscapes with music, sculpt memories with clay. For every story you share, you illuminate a corner of your soul, inviting others to dance in the symphony of your existence.

*"Threads of Tales: A Symphony of Stories"*

Stories, whispers woven into thread,
Tapestries of feeling, where lives are spread.
They dance on tongues, in laughter and sighs,
Emotions' orchestra, reflected in the eyes.

Music's brushstrokes, on melodies they glide,
Sculpting memories, where tears and laughter hide.
Each tale a compass, guiding hearts astray,
Toward solace, wisdom, and the break of day.

In whispered myths, in legends whispered low,
Ancestor's secrets, where ancient spirits flow.
Through fairy tales, where dreams take flight anew,
We glimpse the magic, just within our view.

For stories offer refuge, safe and warm,
A shared embrace, weathering life's harshest storm.
They bridge the chasms, hearts with hearts entwine,
In choruses of laughter, tears that intertwine.

For stories hold the power for soul to ignite,
To heal the broken wand and set shadows right.
They build a bridge, where souls freely roam,
And find their way back, the place called home.

~

# Passions and Affections

Let your heart be a volcano, your spirit a roaring flame! Passions are the driving force of your poem, the embers that keep the fires of creation burning. Whether it's the fiery pursuit of justice, the quiet dedication to craft, or the unyielding love for another soul, hold onto your passions. They are the ink that gives your verses weight, the melody that makes your poem sing.

*"Passions Unleashed: The Fire Within"*

Let us delve deeper, embrace the heat,
Where heart-forged passions forge and meet.
A blazing sun within your breast,
A firefly dance, defying rest.

For passions are the lifeblood's tide,
A restless current, deep inside.
They roar in righteous anger's flame,
Or whisper soft, a yearning name.

Justice: a tempest's righteous wrath,
Against the chains that bind a path.
With fist held high, and voice aflame,
To chase away the shadows' shame.

Craft: a patient, gentle hum,
Where fingers weave, and dreams succumb
To chisel's stroke, or brush's kiss,
To shape a world, from nothingness.

Love: a supernova's blinding might,
A consuming ember, burning bright.
In whispered vows, and gaze entwined,
Two souls ignite, in fire combined.

Yet passions, wild and untamed,
Can blaze out of control, unnamed.
Jealousy's green, devouring shade,
Or fury's grip, a soul betrayed.

So, wield them wisely, these burning coals,
With mindful hand, and open goals.
Let reason temper passion's spark,
To guide the flames and leave their mark.

For ink, when fuelled by fiery soul,
Will paint emotions, make them whole.
Words take flight, on passion's wings,
And verses dance, like whispered things.

So, sing, in thunder or in sigh,
Let every note, on canvas lie.
Embrace the tremor, let it bloom,
paint your passions, in life's grand room.

~

## The Flames of Desire: Exploring the Driving Forces of Passion

Deep within us flicker the flames of desire, driving our ambitions and fuelling our pursuits. This potent force, born from yearning, transforms mere existence into a dance of purpose. Passion acts as the crucible, the fiery workshop where desires take shape, forged into the tools that carve our unique paths.

But finding our true passions demands introspection. We must descend into the caverns of our own souls, asking ourselves what stirs our emotions, what ignites our fury, what whispers mysteries, and what urges us to create. Once identified, these embers need nurturing. Immerse yourself in the fuel of your passion - read, listen, create, and surround yourself with kindred spirits who fan your flames and offer support.

Remember, the crucible of passion is not a haven of comfort. Challenges will come, but embrace them as trials that refine your focus and strengthen your resolve. Each hurdle overcome adds fuel to your fire, making your passion burn brighter and your purpose more robust.

Ultimately, the symphony of desire is a solo concert, yet its melody resonates with the world. Listen to your own song, dance to your own rhythm, and never let the embers within die. For it is in the pursuit of your passionate purpose that you truly come alive, leaving an indelible mark on the world and enriching it with the vibrant hues of your soul.

*"Embers of Purpose: Igniting the Soul's Symphony"*

In caverns deep, where shadows play,
A potent flame begins its sway.
Desire's whispers, soft and keen,
Kindle embers, yet unseen.

A yearning pulse, a restless core,
Drives the soul to seek its door.
What stirs the heart, a tempest's call?
What whispers wisdom, secrets tall?

In introspection's quiet space,
Unmask the truth, reveal the face.
Of passion's spark, a burning need,
To paint, to sing, to plant, to plead.

Then fan the embers, feed the fire,
With words that soar, with brush afire.
Immerse yourself in kindred light,
Where souls ignite, and dreams take flight.

Fear not the forge, the trials' sting,
For challenges, like anvils, ring.
Each test refines, a sculptor's hand,
Forging purpose, strong and grand.

A solo song, yet one that weaves,
Through lives it touches, lives it leaves.
dance with your truth, let passions flare,
Embrace the symphony what you bear.

Leave your mark, as a vibrant hue,
Enrich the world and start anew.
For in the heat of soul set free,
You may find wings, eternally.

~

## Chasing Fireflies: Identifying and Nurturing Our Passions

Within us flicker tiny sparks, like fireflies waiting to ignite. These are our passions, the driving forces that imbue life with purpose and meaning. But unlike the fleeting glow of a firefly, our passions can blaze into a bonfire, illuminating not only our own paths but the world around us.

Discovering these sparks is an adventure. We must delve into our souls, asking what sends shivers of excitement down our spines, what activities make us feel energized even when challenging, what mysteries beckon us to unravel. Once we identify these sparks, we must nurture them.

Immerse yourself in the fuel of your passion. Read, listen, create, and surround yourself with the works of those who have walked similar paths. Consistent practice is key, whether it's penning the first stroke on a blank page or taking the first tentative step towards a daunting goal. Remember, passion thrives on action.

But don't walk this path alone. Seek out kindred spirits who share your fire, their support and collaboration fanning your flames. Remember, challenges are not embers to extinguish, but trials that refine your focus and strengthen your resolve. Each hurdle adds fuel to the fire, making your passion burn brighter and your purpose more robust.

The pursuit of passion isn't about accolades or recognition, it's about the dance with the flames, the journey itself. It's about leaving your mark on the world, not through grand gestures, but through the quiet glow of your unique fire. So chase those fireflies, embrace the sparks within, and let them guide you towards a vibrant, purposeful life that is truly your own.

*"Nurturing the Fire Within"*

In whispers deep, where shadows cling,
Tiny sparks begin to sing.
Passion's embers, faint and frail,
Yearn to dance and cast their trail.

Not fleeting fireflies, but flames,
To light the path, defy the blames.
Seek them out, in heart's own hold,
Where dreams take flight, and stories unfold.

What sends a shiver down your spine,
A thrill that makes the hours align.
What whispers secrets, yearns to fly,
And draws you in, beneath the sky?

Once found, these sparks, so gently tend,
With ink and brush, with voice that lends.
A melody to those dreams' unseen,
A symphony of what dream has been.

Immerse yourself, let passions feed,
On words that bloom, on fertile seed.
Surround your soul with kindred souls,
Whose flames ignite and make you whole.

Fear not the trials, shadows cast,
For challenges refine, make passions last.
Each hurdle crossed, a fuel to burn,
A brighter fire, a purpose earned.

Not accolades, nor fleeting praise,
But in the dance, the vibrant maze,
Of chasing dreams with heart ablaze,
You leave your mark, in countless ways.

So let your fireflies take flight,
Embrace the embers, burning bright.
For in their glow, your path is clear,
A vibrant life held ever dear.

~

## Blossoming Bonds: The Gentle Touch of Affections

In the intricate tapestry of human existence, the threads that bind us most preciously are not those of power, ambition, or fleeting desires. But rather, they are the delicate, yet unyielding threads of affection – love, empathy, and connection. These are the silent whispers that mend broken hearts, the laughter that paints the shadows with light, and the invisible hands that lift us when we stumble.

For within the gentle touch of a hand, the whispered secrets shared under starry skies, the quiet acts of kindness that bloom unnoticed, lies a magic more potent than any spell. It is the magic of belonging, of knowing that we are not alone in this vast universe, that our joys are amplified and our sorrows cushioned by the shared tapestry of human experience.

Affection's strength lies in its quiet resilience. It is the anchor that holds us steady in the storms of life, the haven where we can seek solace and understanding. In the warmth of a loved one's embrace, we find validation and comfort, a reminder that even in the darkest of nights, a star still shines somewhere, a fire still burns.

But affection is not merely a shield, it is also a springboard. It fuels our dreams, inspires our creativity, and pushes us to become the best versions of ourselves. In the eyes of those who love us, we see possibilities, not limitations. We find the courage to climb mountains and cross oceans, fuelled by the knowledge that we are not venturing into the unknown alone.

*"Threads of Gold: A Tapestry of Love"*

Threads of gold, not spun of might,
Weave a tapestry, warm and bright.
Not threads of power, coldly wrought,
But those of love, with kindness fraught.

A gentle touch, a whispered word,
A hand outstretched, unheard, unheard,

Yet seen by hearts, in shadows dim,
These silent threads, they lift and hymn.

Laughter's brush, on canvas vast,
Paints joy's embrace, that shadows cast,
From sunlit peaks to valleys deep,
Love's symphony, in whispers steep.

For in the tide of humankind,
A solace born, a haven we find.
Though storms may rage, and waves may toss,
Affection's anchor holds us close.

A starlit sky, a shared embrace,
In depths of eyes, we find our place.
Not bound by chains, but silken cord,
To dreams we soar, on wings outpoured.

For love's soft light, it fuels the spark,
To climb the heights and leave our mark.
In kindred eyes, our strength we see,
To cross the seas, and wild and free.

So let us weave, with gentle hand,
This tapestry, across the land.
With threads of gold, and whispered song,
Let love prevail, where we belong.

~

Weave threads of love, empathy, and connection into the fabric of your canvas. For the human heart is not an island, but a continent linked by invisible bridges. Reach out, touch, feel the warmth of another soul, the echo of your own laughter in another's voice. Each bond forged, each love shared, adds a vibrant new colour to your palette, enriches the symphony of your existence.

# Regeneration

Just as nature renews itself, so too does the human mind possess the innate potential for regeneration. This section explores the various facets of our resilience; the ability to heal from emotional wounds, learn from setbacks, and emerge stronger. Remember, even the sun sets to rise again. Even the starkest winter yields to the bloom of spring. The human spirit, like the poet's pen, possesses the power of regeneration. This poem, your life, is not etched in stone. Let sorrow flow like cleansing rain, let mistakes be the charcoal that sharpens your lines. For within every scar lies the seed of renewal, every tear a baptism for a stronger, more vibrant verse.

Like the earth that slumbers under winter's frost only to erupt in a riot of spring wildflowers, the human spirit holds an innate power of regeneration. We are not static monuments, etched in stone, but living poems, ever-evolving, ever-renewing. Just as the setting sun promises a dawn, so too can our darkest wounds become fertile ground for growth.

Let sorrow flow like cleansing rain, washing away the dust of pain and leaving behind the fertile soil of resilience. Embrace mistakes as the charcoal that sharpens your lines, the dissonance that leads to a deeper harmony. Within every scar lies the seed of renewal, every tear a baptism for a stronger, more vibrant verse.

This journey of regeneration, however, is not a lone trek through a barren landscape. It is a dance with shadows and light, a symphony played on the strings of acceptance, forgiveness, and unwavering self-belief. In the echoes of past challenges, we learn the wisdom that shapes our future. In the embrace of loved ones, we find the strength to rise again.

So let us shed the skin of despair and step into the sunlit arena of renewal. Let us celebrate the cracks in our pavement, for they are where wildflowers push through. Let us find poetry in the ashes of our trials, for even phoenixes rise from flames. In the symphony of human resilience, every scar becomes a note, every tear a verse, and every setback a bridge to a stronger, more vibrant tomorrow.

*"Resilience's Symphony: Rising from Ashes"*

From frozen earth, where slumber clings,
Awakens fire, in whispers' wings.
Not granite cold, but living rhyme,
The human spirit, born of time.

Sun's gold descends, yet paints the east,
So rise we too, from sorrow's feast.
Let tears like rain, on parched ground fall,
Nurturing strength, within us all.

Mistakes, like charcoal, dark and sharp,
Refine the lines, on life's vast map.
Embrace the stumbles, discord's sting,
For harmony from chaos springs.

Each scar, a story etched in ink,
Each tear, a baptism, at the brink.
Renewed we rise, from ashes' hold,
A vibrant verse, in courage told.

No lonely dance, in barren plight,
But hands entwined, beneath the light.
Acceptance sings, forgiveness blooms,
Self-belief, a sunlit room.

From whispers past, wisdom takes flight,
Loved ones' embrace, our guiding light.
Cast off despair's worn, tattered cloak,
Step bold and free, where shadows broke.

In cracked pavement, wildflowers climb,
Hope's phoenix, born of trials, time.
Each scar, a note, in life's grand song,
Each tear, a verse, where we belong.

So let us rise, with branches bare,
And bloom anew, with sunlit air.
For in the symphony of hearts,
Human resilience plays its part.

~

## Nature's Symphony of Renewal

Where sun scorched earth and winds once hissed,
A silent seed, in slumber kissed.
Beneath the dust, a promise hid,
To paint the scars with desert's pride.

Then rains descend, a whispered grace,
And life awakes, with vibrant face.
Wildflowers push, through parched terrain,
A rainbow dance, where hope has lain.

So let your heart, like sun-baked ground,
Find hidden strength, where roots are found.
From barren cracks, let beauty break,
A fragile bloom, for sorrow's sake.

~

"Nature's Symphony of Renewal" is a poetic exploration of the cyclical journey of life, drawing inspiration from the transformative processes observed in the natural world. Depicting a desolate landscape, scorched by the sun and marked by the whispers of the wind. Within this harsh environment, a dormant seed lies in slumber, carrying with it a silent promise to bring renewal to the scars of the desert. As rains descend, a gentle and whispered grace, life is stirred from its dormancy. The idea of wildflowers pushing through the once parched terrain symbolizes the vibrant and hopeful resurgence of life. The poem encourages to find parallels between the sun-baked ground and their own heart, suggesting that hidden strengths can be discovered where roots are found.

The emergence of beauty from barren cracks becomes a metaphor for the capacity to bloom even in the face of sorrow. Ultimately, "Nature's Symphony of Renewal" invites reflection on resilience and the potential for growth and transformation, drawing inspiration from the intricate dance of life found in the natural world.

## Phoenix Flight

In smouldering ashes, dreams lie curled,
Whispers of fire, in a shattered world.
But from the pyre, a legend takes flight,
A phoenix born, in embers' light.

With wings of gold, it tears the night,
Soaring above, on dawn's first light.
Transformed by flame, its spirit sings,
A testament to hope, on broken wings.

So, rise you too, from ashes deep,
Where trials burn, and shadows creep.
Embrace the change, the fiery test,
And soar anew, from sorrow's nest.

~

Mind delves into the transformative power of resilience, drawing parallels between the phoenix's legendary rebirth and the human capacity to rise from the ashes of adversity. Begin with the vivid idea of dreams smouldering in ashes, capturing a sense of loss and shattered aspirations. However, from this desolation, the phoenix emerges as a symbol of hope, ignited by the remaining embers. The transformation brought about by the flames is likened to a spirited song, emphasizing the resilience and strength found in the face of challenges.

The call to rise from the deep ashes, where trials burn and shadows creep, serves as an encouragement to embrace change and undergo the fiery test of adversity. The concluding lines beautifully encapsulate the essence of the poem, urging readers to soar anew from the nest of sorrow, emphasizing the potential for growth and renewal even during challenges. "In Ember's Embrace" celebrates the human spirit's ability to find hope and strength amid the ruins of shattered dreams.

## Daybreak's Embrace

Night's curtain falls, on whispered sighs,
Stars fade to grey, as darkness lies.
But hold your breath, for in the east,
A promise sleeps, a silent feast.

A single spark, on horizon's rim,
Ignites the world, with hope's first hymn.
Sun's golden fingers, chase away gloom,
Painting the sky, with vibrant bloom.

So let your spirit, wake with dawn,
Renewed by dreams when hope is born.
In darkness deep, let faith ignite,
And greet the day, with radiant light.

~

The thought captures the evocative imagery of the transition from night to the day, weaving a poetic narrative of hope and renewal. With the symbolic fall of Night's curtain, describing stars fading and darkness lying. This sets a contemplative atmosphere, emphasizing the quiet moments before the promise of a new day unfolds. The anticipation builds with the mention of a promise sleeping in the east, creating a sense of expectation and potential. The metaphor of a single spark on the horizon's rim signifies the beginning of dawn, heralding the gradual illumination of the world. The idea of the Sun's golden fingers chasing away gloom and painting the sky with vibrant bloom portrays the transformative power of sunlight and the birth of hope.

The thought concludes with an empowering call to let one's spirit wake with dawn, emphasizing renewal through dreams and the ignition of faith in the face of darkness. The metaphor of greeting the day with radiant light conveys the idea of embracing positivity and optimism as each new day begins.

## Chiselled Soul

A rough-hewn block, untamed and wild,
Holds whispers yet, of beauty mild.
The sculptor's hand, with gentle art,
Reveals the form, within the heart.

With hammer's song, and chisel's kiss,
A hidden grace begins to miss.
Lines carved deep, in shadows cast,
A story etched that holds the past.

So let your wounds, like stone untamed,
Be shaped by time, by lessons claimed.
Through pain's harsh blows, let beauty rise,
A sculpted soul, beneath your eyes.

~

A poignant thought that draws on the metaphor of a rough-hewn block to convey the essence of personal growth and resilience. The imagery of an untamed and wild block symbolizes the raw and unexplored potential within an individual. The sculptor's hand, portrayed with gentle art, represents the transformative power of time, experience, and introspection. The idea that each person carries whispers of hidden beauty within, waiting to be revealed through the sculpting process of life. The hammer's song and chisel's kiss evoke the challenges and experiences that shape and molds an individual.

The carved lines deep in shadows cast reflect the narrative of one's past, acknowledging the scars and stories that contribute to the unique sculpture of the soul. Mindset encourages embracing wounds and challenges as part of the sculpting process, allowing them to be shaped by time and claimed as valuable lessons. Through pain's harsh blows, the poem suggests that beauty can rise, portraying a vision of a sculpted soul that emerges beneath one's eyes and encourages resilience, growth, and the acknowledgment of beauty in the midst of life's sculpting process.

## Dissonance Transformed

Strings sing off-key, a tangled tune,
Discordant notes, beneath the moon.
But patient hands, with practiced grace,
Weave chaos into vibrant space.

The melody unfolds, from clashing strings,
A harmony, where sorrow clings.
In minor tones, a story plays,
Of battles fought, and brighter days.

So let your heart, a symphony untold,
Embrace the notes, both harsh and bold.
From dissonance, let music rise,
A testament to strength, beneath your eyes.

~

"Dissonance Transformed" intricately weaves a metaphorical tapestry where life's challenges are compared to a musical composition. The initial scene portrays strings singing off-key, a tangled and discordant tune beneath the moon. However, the narrative takes a hopeful turn as patient hands, guided by practiced grace, skilfully transform chaos into vibrant space.

The unfolding melody mirrors the resilience found in facing adversity. Through the metaphorical minor tones, the poem tells a story of battles fought and the anticipation of brighter days. The interplay of dissonance and harmony becomes a metaphor for life's journey, where challenges are essential components in the symphony of our existence.

In the concluding lines encourage to embrace the heart's untold symphony, acknowledging both the harsh and bold notes. The thought beautifully suggests that through life's dissonance, one can compose a testament to inner strength, creating a unique and powerful melody.

## Light and Shadow's Blend

On canvas bare, a darkness sleeps,
Where secrets hide, and silence weeps.
But brushstrokes dance, with hues unseen,
A tapestry of what has been.

Light pierces through, in golden streaks,
Where shadows play, and beauty speaks.
A depth unfolds, on canvas vast,
A story told that shadows cast.

So let your life, a canvas be,
Where darkness weaves, with harmony.
In every shade, where truth reside.
A masterpiece, with shadows tied.

~

"Light and Shadow's Blend" paints a vivid picture of life as an evolving masterpiece on a canvas. The context begins with a canvas bare, symbolizing the uncharted territories of existence where secrets and silence reside. However, the narrative takes a turn as brushstrokes dance, creating a tapestry of unseen hues.

The interplay of light and shadow becomes central to the metaphor, with light piercing through the darkness in golden streaks. This juxtaposition allows shadows to play and beauty to speak, unveiling a depth on the vast canvas of life. The shadows, far from being mere darkness, become an integral part of the unfolding story that invites you to view their lives as a canvas where darkness and light harmonize. In every shade, the truth resides, and the shadows are not adversaries but essential components of the masterpiece. "Light and Shadow's Blend" beautifully encapsulates the idea that life's canvas gains richness and depth through the seamless integration of both light and shadow.

## The Fisherman's Heart

Old scars of nets, upon his hands,
Whispered tales, of windswept sands.
Storms faced and calmed, beneath the sun,
A weathered soul, a battle won.

He tells of waves, that tossed and drowned,
Of depths explored, where fears were found.
But in his eyes, a fire glows,
A testament to what one knows.

So let your scars, like stories told,
Be badges worn, from journeys bold.
In every mark, a lesson lies,
The echoes strong, of weathered skies.

~

"The Fisherman's Heart" paints a poignant portrait of a seasoned fisherman and the stories etched upon his weathered hands. The context begins by describing the old scars on the fisherman's hands, suggesting a lifetime of experiences and challenges. These scars become silent narrators of tales from windswept sands, storms faced and conquered beneath the sun. Further delves into the fisherman's stories of waves that tossed and drowned, and the depths explored where fears were confronted. Despite the hardships, there's a resilient spirit within him, symbolized by the glowing fire in his eyes – a testament to the wisdom gained through lived experiences.

The poem concludes with a universal message, urging readers to embrace their scars as stories told and badges earned from bold journeys. Each mark becomes a lesson, and within them lie the echoes of weathered skies. "The Fisherman's Heart" beautifully captures the essence of resilience, wisdom, and the transformative power of life's journey.

## The Dancer's Triumph

A broken heel, a stage in tears,
Shattered dreams, and whispered fears.
But through the pain, a spirit burns,
To rise again, where sorrow yearns.

With bandaged foot, and trembling hand,
She takes the stage, a promised land.
Each step a whisper, soft and slow,
A testament to what we know.

So let your falls, be moments traced,
Where strength is found, in hearts embraced.
Though stumbles come, and shadows creep,
The dancer's soul will surely take a leap.

~

"The Dancer's Triumph" captures the resilience and indomitable spirit of a dancer who faces setbacks and challenges. The context begins by describing the broken heel, a stage in tears, shattered dreams, and whispered fears, a portrayal of the hardships and obstacles the dancer encounters. However, amidst the pain, there's an unwavering spirit that burns within, yearning to rise again.

The narrative unfolds with the dancer, despite a bandaged foot and trembling hand, taking the stage as a promised land. Each step becomes a soft and slow whisper, serving as a testament to the strength inherent in the human spirit.

The thought concludes with a universal message, encouraging readers to see their own falls as moments traced, where strength is found, and hearts are embraced. Despite stumbles and creeping shadows, the dancer's soul takes a leap, symbolizing the triumph over adversity. "The Dancer's Triumph" captures the theme of resilience, perseverance, and the transformative power of overcoming challenges.

## The Writer's Rebirth

Pages torn, and ink stained tears,
Tell tales of doubt, and hidden fears.
The empty page, a canvas vast,
Haunted whispers from the past.

But fingers trace, a single line,
A thread of hope, in starlight's shine.
Words take flight, on wings of dawn,
A story born, where darkness wanes.

So let your wounds, be fertile ground,
Where new beginnings can be found.
From shattered ink, let stories bloom,
The writer's spirit overcomes the gloom.

~

"The Writer's Rebirth" beautifully encapsulates the journey grappling with doubts and fears. The context begins by describing the pages as torn and stained with ink, symbolizing the struggles and emotional challenges faced by the writer. The empty page is likened to a vast canvas haunted by whispers from the past. Further takes a turn as the fingers trace a single line, a thread of hope illuminated by starlight. Words then take flight on wings of dawn, signifying the emergence of a new narrative where darkness begins to wane.

The concluding lines carry a powerful message, encourages to see wounds as fertile ground for new beginnings. From the shattered ink, stories bloom, emphasizing the resilience of the writer's spirit that triumphs over the gloom. "The Writer's Rebirth" is a poetic exploration of the transformative nature of creativity and the ability to find hope and renewal amid challenges.

# Embracing the Whole Canvas:

Imagine life as a vast canvas, not a sterile expanse of white, but a vibrant tapestry woven with threads of every shade. This is the essence of "embracing the whole canvas," a philosophy that celebrates the entirety of our existence, from the sun-drenched peaks of passionate pursuits to the moonlit valleys of sorrow and vulnerability. Within us flicker flames, tiny sparks yearning to ignite. These are our passions – the fiery urges that drive us to create, connect, and chase dreams. Embracing the whole canvas entails nurturing these flames, feeding them with experiences, learning, and the courage to express ourselves authentically. It's about revelling in the exhilaration of artistic creation, the warmth of shared laughter, and the thrill of pushing boundaries, even when the path is uncertain.

Yet, the canvas is not a realm of perpetual sunshine. Life's storms leave their mark, etching cracks and shadows onto our tapestry. Scars, tears, and moments of hardship weave their own threads into the narrative. Embracing the whole canvas means acknowledging these darker hues, not with shame or denial, but with acceptance and understanding. The stumbles, the losses, and the moments of doubt are not detours, but brushstrokes that add depth and texture to the story. They inform our resilience, shape our compassion, and remind us of the preciousness of joy.

*"A Canvas of Life: Threads of Every Hue"*

On a vast expanse, not sterile white,
But threads of every hue ignite,
A tapestry of life, a vibrant whole,
Where shadows dance and passions stroll.

Tiny flames within, like embers glow,
Dreams take flight, where colors flow.
Brushstrokes bold, on canvas grand,
In laughter's light, a helping hand.

Sunlit peaks, where spirits soar,
Chasing dreams, forevermore.
But storms will rage, and skies grow dim,
Leaving scars, a whisper grim.

Tears may fall, like silvered thread,
Woven in, where shadows spread.
Yet hold them close, these darker hues,
For depths unfold, where wisdom brews.

Each stumble etched, a brushstroke true,
Building strength, in shades of blue.
For shattered heart, a lesson learned,
Compassion's flame, in sorrow burned.

Embrace the whole, with open eye,
The moonlit vale, the sunlit sky.
No masterpiece, but stories spun,
In every thread, a life begun.

So let your canvas, vibrant be,
With tears and laughter, wild and free.
Embrace the whole, with gentle grace,
This masterpiece, your life's embrace.

~

## A Manifesto for living in the "Canvas of the Mind"

Within the hushed chambers of our minds lies a hidden atelier, an infinite canvas where possibilities dance and dreams take flight. This is our manifesto, not etched in stone but whispered in the rustle of thoughts, a celebration of living in the vibrant tapestry of our own consciousness. Here, amongst the constellations of memories and the nebulae of emotions, we craft a masterpiece, brushstroke by brushstroke, hue by hue.

This is not an escape from the world, but rather a dive into its very essence. Within these swirling galaxies of ideas lies the power to understand, to empathize, to shape our narratives into symphonies of purpose and passion. We become architects of our own existence, moulding the clay of experience and moulding it with the chisel of imagination. The boundaries blur, reality bending to the whispers of our inner voices, transforming into a kaleidoscope of possibilities.

Yet, this canvas is not a sterile utopia. Cracks will appear, shadows will linger, and storms will rage. We are not called to erase these, but to embrace them as the shades that give depth to our tapestry. The tears, the losses, the doubts – these are not flaws, but the charcoal that sharpens our lines, the dissonance that leads to deeper harmony. They remind us of the preciousness of the light, weaving resilience into the very fabric of our souls.

Ultimately, this manifesto is a call to awaken the artist within. We are not bound by the confines of the everyday, but empowered to paint our lives with vibrant strokes of colour. Let curiosity be our palette, experiences our pigments, and mistakes our playful splatters. Let every scar be a testament to our strength, every tear a baptism for a bolder hue. In this vast atelier of the mind, every emotion, every thought, every whisper contributes to the masterpiece that is our existence.

So, let us raise our brushes, dip them deep into the wellspring of our being, and splash our dreams onto the canvas of our lives. It is a journey without end, a dance with the ever-changing currents of our consciousness. But in this boundless creation, in this embrace of the whole canvas, we find not only meaning, but the very essence of who we are, forever evolving, forever becoming, an eternal masterpiece whispered in the symphony of our minds. Namaste!

*"Whispers on the Canvas: A Manifesto of the Mind's Masterpiece"*

In hushed chambers, where whispers ignite,
Lies a canvas, an infinite night.
Not of linen, nor stone-etched decree,
But the boundless expanse of the mind, you see.

Here, constellations of memories gleam,
Nebulae of emotions, a swirling stream.
We are architects, crafting our days,
With brushstrokes of hopes, in a vibrant maze.

This manifesto, not carved in the stone,
Whispers in thoughts, where dreams are sown.
Not an escape from the world's loud strife,
But a dive to its core, where lessons give life.

Galaxies of ideas, in swirling flight,
Empower us to understand, to empathize, with all our might.
Boundaries blur, as whispers take hold,
Reality bends, a story untold.

The canvas, though vibrant, knows darkness well,
Cracks that whisper, shadows that dwell.
Tears are not stains, but a charcoal's might,
Sharpening lines, in the moonlit night.

Losses and doubts, not flaws to erase,
But dissonance leading to harmony's grace.

Resilience woven, in threads of despair,
Each scar a testament, a strength we wear.

This manifesto, a call to the soul,
To awaken the artist, make ourselves whole.
Curiosity, our palette, vibrant and vast,
Experiences, pigments, that stories surpass.

Mistakes, playful splatters, on life's grand art,
Each scar a testament, a beating heart.
Let emotions and whispers find their hue,
Contribute to the symphony, ever new.

So, raise your brush, dip deep in your soul,
Splash dreams on the canvas, make stories unfold.
A journey unending, a dance in the mind,
Embrace the whole canvas, the masterpiece you find.

For in this boundless creation, we truly belong,
Forever evolving, in life's endless song.
A whisper, a symphony, our minds' grand design,
The eternal masterpiece, forever thine.

~

# About the Author

Rajesh is a technologist, advisor, author and key note speaker with over three decades of accomplished experience in Information Technology (IT) domain, A diversified background in in the areas of IT infrastructure, Cloud computing, emerging technologies such as AI/ML and Data Engineering and Open source systems and is a certified ISO27K lead auditor and Project management professional.

On personal front he has authored several blogs, articles and published many books on technology, short stories, poetry in Marathi, Hindi and English, besides he is a social activist, foodie, photographer and loves long drives and farming. He is based out of Bangalore, India

rajesh_dangi@yahoo.com

Twitter: @rajesh_dangi

www.ingramcontent.com/pod-product-compliance
Lightning Source LLC
LaVergne TN
LVHW041104150826
845673LV00007B/1921

* 9 7 9 8 8 9 2 3 3 7 0 1 4 *